CORNERSTONE OF LIBERTY

PROPERTY RIGHTS IN 21ST-CENTURY AMERICA

CORNERSTONE OF LIBERTY

PROPERTY RIGHTS IN 21ST-CENTURY AMERICA

TIMOTHY SANDEFUR

CATO INSTITUTE
WASHINGTON, D.C.

Library of Congress Cataloging-in-Publication Data

Sandefur, Timothy.
    Cornerstone of liberty : property rights in 21st century America / Timothy Sandefur.
        p. cm.
    Includes bibliographical references and index.
    ISBN 1-930865-96-1 (paper : alk. paper) -- ISBN 1-930865-97-X (cloth : alk. paper)
    1. Right of property--United States. I. Title.

KF562.S26 2006
346.7304'2--dc22   2006040644

Cover design by Jon Meyers.
Printed in the United States of America.

CATO INSTITUTE
1000 Massachusetts Ave., N.W.
Washington, D.C. 20001
www.cato.org

*This book is gratefully dedicated
to my colleagues at the*
Pacific Legal Foundation
*who, for more than 30 years,
have been at the forefront of defending private property rights
in courts across the country.*

Contents

Acknowledgments

I would like to thank the many people who offered their advice and assistance on this project, particularly the Cato Institute's David Boaz, Tom G. Palmer, and Roger Pilon, who offered many helpful suggestions; my PLF colleagues James S. Burling, Deborah J. La Fetra, and R. S. Radford; the Institute for Justice's Scott Bullock, who argued the *Kelo* case before the Supreme Court; my friend Scott Cueto; my father Mark Sandefur; law student Fern Richardson; and most of all, Erin McCarty, who gave me time and patience to get the project done on time. I love you, Erin.

1. Introduction

What is it about our homes that makes them more than just wood and bricks? When Hurricane Katrina slammed into New Orleans and Mississippi in 2005, leaving thousands homeless, the nation saw firsthand just how much our property really means to us. In a commentary on National Public Radio's *Morning Edition*, New Orleans schoolteacher Anne Rochell Konigsmark described how it felt to lose her home. She appreciated the hospitality of the Atlanta relatives who took her in, she said, and Atlanta was very pretty. But it wasn't *home*, and she kept thinking about what she had left behind. "I imagine my house, which did not flood, sitting on our deserted street, hot and silent, rotten food in the fridge, toys and knickknacks gathering dust. I often dial my home phone number. The voice mail no longer picks up. It just rings and rings. I worry that someday, someone will answer."[1]

Private property is an essential part of the human experience. Its importance to us is embodied in silly, sentimental poems like Edgar Guest's "Home" ("It takes a heap o' livin' in a house t' make it home") and in our most eloquent literary expressions, such as *The Odyssey*, in which the Greek warrior Odysseus braves all the wild dangers of legend to reach his "grand and gracious house."[2] Not only are our homes important; business owners, too, find profound personal meaning in private property. They treasure the feeling of self-sufficiency and independence that comes from owning and operating their own shops or restaurants. As writer and businessman James Chan explains, entrepreneurs "are people who feel compelled to express our individuality through running our own businesses."[3] Personal possessions, too, are obvious examples of the importance of private property in our lives; anyone who owns a wedding ring, or a photo album, or a piece of heirloom furniture knows the immense personal meaning that owned objects can embody—a personal meaning we call "sentimental value." People who have suffered a robbery or a burglary can attest to the terrible consequences of property crime; the shock and intense feelings of personal violation stay with victims long afterwards.

Property isn't important just for individuals; it's also an essential ingredient for economic growth and prosperity, for secure savings and intelligent investment, and for the sophisticated transactions that raise the standard of living for everybody in society. Property enables people to organize their resources and work together, to experiment with innovations, and to reap the rewards of their hard work. During the 20th century, many misguided political leaders tried to abolish private property, and the results were disasters in every conceivable way. Those societies lost everything, from social prosperity and peace to the very notion of personal privacy.

America's Founding Fathers well understood the centrality of property rights for any stable, successful, virtuous society. "That alone is a *just* government," wrote James Madison, "which *impartially* secures to every man, whatever is his *own*."[4] But during the 20th century, political and legal thinkers came to reject the lessons the Founders taught us and to denigrate the importance of private property rights. Property, they argued, is really created by society or government rather than by individuals. Government should solve social problems, therefore, by taking property from people who have it and giving it to those who do not, or by giving the government the authority to control the use of property held by individual owners. As those ideas gained hold in the United States, property owners became increasingly burdened by laws that tell them what they may do with their property or impose exhausting bureaucratic requirements whenever they want to use their land. In many cases, government even takes their homes or belongings outright. As an attorney at the Pacific Legal Foundation—America's oldest public interest law foundation dedicated to protecting private property rights and other individual liberties—I've been in a unique position to observe some of the more disturbing ways in which government violates the fundamental rights of Americans to acquire, use, and trade property. Such interference curtails the essential freedoms that Americans ought to be able to take for granted, and often the consequences are terrible: injustice, economic stagnation, and the erosion of the fundamental basis of healthy democracy.

In 2005 the U.S. Supreme Court decided the case of *Kelo v. New London*, holding that government may use eminent domain to condemn private homes and transfer the land to developers who want

2

to demolish and replace the homes with privately owned shopping malls, hotels, or convention centers. The decision sparked a national outcry, and political leaders began looking for ways to solve the problem. But the abuse of eminent domain is only one aspect of a property rights crisis in America today. Addressing that crisis requires understanding the origin and meaning of property rights, as well as the role of those rights in the U.S. Constitution. In what follows, I will give a brief account of why property rights matter— to human beings generally and to Americans in particular. I will then look at the state of property rights in our nation today. Finally, I will discuss some ways to better protect this most important of all human rights. Throughout, I provide some startling examples of government's abuse of property rights, drawn mostly from cases in which the Pacific Legal Foundation has worked to defend property owners. Because this essay is intended only as a brief introduction to recent controversies over the security of private property, I have skipped over many important and complicated aspects of property rights. Those who wish to pursue these issues further will find some reading suggestions in the bibliography.

2. Why Property Rights Are Important

Frank Bugryn and his three elderly siblings owned two houses and a Christmas tree farm in Bristol, Connecticut. The family had lived on the 32-acre homestead for more than 60 years when city officials decided that their land would produce more tax revenue if it were owned by the Yarde Metals Corporation instead. Because the property was next to a state highway, the company hoped to construct a large sign and entranceway to attract more business. But the Bugryns refused to sell, so the city used its eminent domain power to condemn their property.

In May 1998 Frank and his family asked a state court to stop the city from condemning their land. The Fifth Amendment to the U.S. Constitution, after all, declares that government may take private property only for a "public use" and only if it pays the owner "just compensation." The Bugryns argued that the taking was, not for a "public use," but for the private use of Yarde Metals. And they didn't want to leave. "I don't want to go anywhere," Frank told the court. "My parents built the family house in 1939, and I built my own house on the property 42 years ago. I'm almost 78. Where am I going to go now?" But Mayor Frank Nicastro testified that the industrial park was "in the best interest of the future growth of the city," because it would "build up the tax base."[1]

The court refused to intervene, holding that the condemnations of the Bugryns' homes "do not . . . constitute serious or material injuries."[2] The Bugryns appealed, and while their case was pending, the community rallied against them; even the nearby newspaper, the *Hartford Courant*, editorialized repeatedly in favor of the city. Finally, the Connecticut Appellate Court decided to allow the condemnation, and the city continued its plans—even though by this time the lawsuit had taken so long that Yarde Metals had given up and moved out of town. The state supreme court declined to take the case, and the Bugryns were ordered to move out.

In 2004, when the family still refused to leave their homes, the city initiated proceedings to evict them. Once again, the *Courant* attacked them in an editorial, calling their resistance a "public farce" and a "melodrama" and denouncing the family for "stall[ing] and draw[ing] upon the public's sympathy."[3] Meanwhile, 76-year-old Michael Dudko, husband of one of the Bugryn sisters and a Polish immigrant who at the age of 15 had been taken from his home by the Nazis and forced into farm labor, suffered a relapse of cancer and died. After a nearby radio station ran a story about the Bugryns' plight, an anonymous, irate telephone call forced the police to post a guard in the mayor's office.[4] Relations within the Bugryn family became strained; when one sister failed to leave her house in time, her nephew took the city's side, telling reporters that "people are pointing the finger at the mayor and the council and city officials, but all they're really doing in taking the property is using an eminent domain system that was given to them by the legislature."[5] The reverberating effects of eminent domain not only disrupted the family and community; they also bred a sense of disillusionment best expressed by Frank Bugryn himself, who told a reporter, "I'm a veteran of World War II, I fought for our freedom, democracy. But it seems 60 years later it doesn't work."[6] Finally, the family was forced to leave their land.

Frank's grandson, Michael Dudko, describes how he felt about the whole experience. "It has become an act of stealing," he writes. "Citizens' private property rights are totally disregarded. You're cheated on the value of what they take. There is dishonesty on the part of elected officials of why they are doing what they are doing. Those freedoms we all talk about on the Fourth of July don't mean much if our government can make a buck off its citizens by nullifying their validity."[7]

Eminent domain—government's power to force a person to sell his home, his business, or other property to the government at a price it deems "just compensation"—is one of the most extreme forms of government coercion, and today among the most common. Used for centuries for constructing railroads, canals, and post offices, eminent domain is now a multi-billion-dollar industry. Governments throughout America routinely seize property to transfer it to private companies to "create jobs" and increase the tax base of a community.[8] In 1999 the city of Merriam, Kansas, condemned a Toyota dealership to sell its land to the BMW dealership next door.[9] That same year a Washington court upheld the city of Bremerton's condemnation of

22 homes to resell the land to private developers.[10] Mesa, Arizona, condemned a profitable brake shop to replace it with a more profitable hardware store.[11] In one especially egregious case, billionaire Donald Trump convinced the government of Atlantic City to condemn the home of an elderly widow so that he could build a limousine parking lot.[12] Although a state court later blocked that condemnation, stories like this are startlingly common, and property owners in such cases rarely manage to keep their land. As attorney Jennifer Kruckeberg writes, "Corporations, using cities as their personal real estate agents, are proposing the following assignment: 'Find me your most prominent location, get rid of what is on it, help me pay for it, and maybe you will be lucky enough to have me move to your city.' Such is the state of the current eminent domain power."[13]

In the 2005 case of *Kelo v. New London*, the U.S. Supreme Court held that the Constitution does not forbid such condemnations, even though the Fifth Amendment requires that takings be for a "public use." Because "promoting economic development is a traditional and long accepted function of government," five justices held that the government is benefiting the public when it transfers property to private businesses for private development.[14] "Public use," the Court declared, means the same thing as "public benefit," and it's up to the legislature or the city council to decide what distribution of property will benefit the public. The decision caused a national outcry, including a formal resolution by the U.S. House of Representatives expressing its "grave disapproval."[15] Many state legislatures began reexamining their eminent domain practices.

But eminent domain is only one of the many ways government deprives us of our property rights. The Fifth Amendment requires government to pay owners "just compensation" when their land is taken from them, yet through a growing array of laws and regulations, government today deprives countless owners of the value of their land—prohibiting them from using it, or selling it, or building on it—without actually forcing them to hand over the deed to the property. Of course, if government could evade the just compensation requirement by using this technical loophole—taking away the *use* of the land but not the land itself—the owners would be left with an empty title and property rights would be all but meaningless. In fact, as early as the 1870s, the Supreme Court held that government could not be allowed take away the use of land "without making

7

any compensation" on the grounds that "in the narrowest sense of that word, it is not *taken* for the public use."[16] Although in some cases the Court requires government to compensate people for these "regulatory takings," in more recent years, it has allowed government to impose more and more such restrictions.

Lake Tahoe, a beautiful resort community straddling the California-Nevada border, is governed by a special agency called the Tahoe Regional Planning Agency. In 1981 the TRPA instituted a "temporary moratorium" on all construction in the Lake Tahoe area to give itself time to study the increasing amount of algae that was polluting the lake's once-clear water. The agency's report, produced in 1984, recommended banning almost all construction in the Tahoe area, but a federal court held that those recommendations would still allow too much development, and it blocked the report's implementation. It wasn't until 1987 that the TRPA produced a new report, recommending that every piece of land in the area be subject to individual assessment for permission to build. But over all that time, the moratorium on construction continued.

Some 700 landowners filed suit against the agency, arguing that it had effectively taken away their property by prohibiting them from using it.[17] What followed was almost two decades of complicated litigation; in 2000 the Ninth Circuit Court of Appeals found that, although the "temporary" moratorium had barred construction for more than a decade, the government did not need to pay just compensation because it had not "taken" the land. Two years later, the U.S. Supreme Court agreed. Justice Stevens, who would also write the *Kelo* decision, held that the ban on construction was only temporary, and thus the landowners (some 300 of whom had actually died by the time the Supreme Court took their case) still might be able to use their property—someday.[18] And in any case, Stevens continued, government takes away so much property from so many people that it can't possibly afford to pay for it. Seriously enforcing the just compensation requirement "would transform government regulation into a luxury few governments could afford . . . [and] render routine government processes prohibitively expensive. . . ."[19] Since government doesn't have the money, it can ignore the Constitution's compensation requirement.

More startling than those stories is the fact that many of today's intellectual leaders—political scientists, lawyers, politicians, and historians—view property rights as unimportant, or as passé. Testifying before the U.S. Senate on the subject of eminent domain months after the *Kelo* case was decided, Thomas Merrill, a law professor who specializes in law and economics at Columbia University, expressed astonishment at the public outcry. He found it "remarkable," he said, "indeed quite stunning," that there was such an "overwhelming reaction" against the *Kelo* decision. It "really sobered me quite a bit," he told the senators.

> I've given a great deal of thought to what it is about the decision that has caused this. . . . And I think there are many explanations, but I think the nub of the problem is that the American people believe that property rights are invested with moral significance. It's not just a measure of value. It's something that people think has an important moral and constitutional dimension.[20]

Many academics regard this belief as a primitive superstition. But the American people are right: property rights *do* have moral significance and a constitutional dimension.

Property is at the heart of many of the most important aspects of human life—from our desire for privacy to our need for fellowship, from our wish to create places where we can be ourselves to our need to provide for the future in case of emergency. It is a central element of virtually every important decision we make in our lives. Little wonder that people think property rights have moral significance. A child who has his toy stolen by a bully understands the moral significance of property. A teenager who buys her first car with her own hard-earned money understands. So, too, does the homeowner who is ordered to give up her family home so that the government can give the land to a private developer to build a convention center, or the family that dreams of building a home on property they've purchased, only to learn that the government refuses to issue a permit.

The experiences of Susette Kelo, the Bugryn family, and many others like them across America are individual episodes in a larger property rights crisis. Property has been a central preoccupation of political and legal thinkers for many centuries, of course, but these examples demonstrate what some philosophers have recognized all along: property is central to our lives as individuals and as a society. Any country that tramples on property rights, that routinely ignores them or violates them, is trifling with one of humanity's primary values.

Property Is Natural

Private property is one of humanity's great discoveries, like fire, or DNA, or the scientific method. Like fire, property has the ability to release a kind of unseen power from nature, to transform a desert like Las Vegas into a luxurious resort, for instance. Like DNA, property represents something deeply ingrained in human nature; no society has ever been found that did not have some concept of property. And, of course, we can ignore what property rights teach us, just as we can ignore the scientific method. But the results won't be good.

The concept of private property is much older than written history. The Greek philosophers Plato and Aristotle debated the role property should play in a society, and in the years since, virtually every political philosopher has discussed the role that property plays in social life. The universality of property suggests immediately that the concept is not just the creation of particular cultures, like a musical style or a language. Instead, property is something common to all human beings *as* human beings—it doesn't have to be taught to people, because it is natural.

Many animals have a sort of personal sphere of privacy—a region around themselves where they don't allow others, or where they allow only a few intimates. This tendency is closely related to the basic drive of any organism to preserve itself from harm and to protect its territory.[21] Human beings, too, naturally develop a concept of "mine" in parallel with their development of self.

Children discover the idea of "mine" very early on, and they seek to exclude others, even their own parents, from things they identify as theirs. Such early development suggests that the concept of "mine" is not initially *taught* to children, or absorbed by them from the surrounding culture, but rather is a natural tendency of humans. Indeed, what children need to be taught is how to *share,* not how to believe in private property rights! A child's "awareness of his own property rights," writes Dr. Benjamin Spock, comes naturally "because it fits with his growing sense of self and assertion of self. Early in his second year he becomes conscious of the fact that his body is *his.*" This explains why many experts on raising children

10

advise parents to take care not to push their children into "sharing" too hard or too fast. "Most children have too great a need to hang on to their own things and too little enjoyment of sharing to be able to yield—even for a few minutes. In fact, I have the impression that when parents make too insistent demands for sharing, it only makes a child more 'selfish.' He feels that not only other children but his parents too are trying to deprive him of his possessions."[22] In some cases, children have been raised in experimental conditions in attemps to avoid exposing them to the concept of "mine"; yet they develop the idea on their own. One such experiment was performed in Israeli communes, called *kibbutzim*, which tried to raise children without a concept of private property. The experiment was a failure; children were "strongly directed toward private ownership" and could only be "gradually weaned" from the idea by relentless conditioning. Some children did finally lose the concept of property, but research suggests that they grew up with a deep sense of alienation and guilt and a reluctance to engage in self-expression and friendship.[23]

A sense of self is a natural need for humans, writes philosopher Daniel Dennett. All animals engage in the "biological principle of distinguishing self from world," but humans engage in this process not only in their physical capacities but in their minds as well.[24] We use the world around us to construct artifacts that expand our personal boundaries over the world, so as to preserve and express ourselves. We do the same thing with our minds: just as spiders spin webs, so each human being "makes a *self*,"[25] not only through the friendships we nourish and the ideas we adopt, but through the things we create and preserve.

The most obvious example of self-expression through private property is the *home*. Our homes are more than buildings; they are projections, and essential components, of our selves. They are ways in which we extend our souls into the physical world. This is why being separated from our homes can be a traumatic experience. "It is commonly observed," writes Dennett,

> that old folks removed from their homes to hospital settings are put at a tremendous disadvantage, even though their basic bodily needs are well provided for. They often *appear* to be quite demented—to be utterly incapable of feeding, clothing, and washing themselves. . . . Often, however, if they

11

are returned to their homes, they can manage quite well for themselves. How do they do this? Over the years, they have loaded their home environments with ultrafamiliar landmarks, triggers for habits, reminders of what to do, where to find the food, how to get dressed, where the telephone is, and so forth. . . . Taking them out of their homes is literally separating them from large parts of their minds—potentially just as devastating a development as undergoing brain surgery.[26]

The home serves as a sort of map or biography of the self, simultaneously a tool and an artwork. What we own doesn't just tell us *about* ourselves; in some ways, it allows us to *be* ourselves in the first place. Humans express themselves through objects, not just in art, but in the homes they decorate, the jewelry they choose to wear, and even the kinds of cars they drive. As Virginia Postrel explains, the things people own allow them to become a part of subcultures with which they feel a connection. "A mid-twentieth-century homemaker who furnished her dining room with Colonial reproductions was engaged not in time travel or archaeology but in self-expression: *I like that. I'm like that.*"[27] This is also true of the personal property we own. We naturally differentiate ourselves from others, or demonstrate our membership in a group, by using property as a cultural signal. We wear buttons or baseball caps with logos that identify us with political causes or musical groups. Without the ability to own and use such objects, our sense of self-definition and self-expression would suffer.

Economists refer to the importance that people ascribe to their property as "sentimental value," a term sometimes used as a pejorative, as if such value were really unimportant. But *all* value is, in some way or another, "sentimental" value, since the price of any object depends only on the needs and desires of people who want to buy or sell it. And sentimental value is one of the most basic sources of economic value: we associate objects with people and ideas and experiences and possibilities that are important to us, and those associations make things precious.

Nobody knows that better than people who have had their property stolen from them. In 1994 Charles Francis Adams of Dover, Massachusetts, suffered a very unusual theft when burglars made off with a family heirloom: the earliest known portrait of Thomas

Jefferson, painted by Mather Brown in 1786 and originally owned by Charles's ancestor, President John Adams.[28] Although the portrait was insured for $500,000, it was really priceless—depicting Jefferson at the age of 43, when he was America's fashionable ambassador to France. The painting was stashed in a concrete-reinforced safe, but thieves pried the safe open, broke through the concrete, and made off with the portrait. It took the Federal Bureau of Investigation two years to find the painting and return it to Adams. "This is a painting that has sentimental value to the Adamses, and it's an important piece of American history," said Adams's spokewoman.[29] But historical value and sentimental value are, essentially, the same thing. The reason antiques, or paintings, or family heirlooms have any value at all is because people treasure their past and invest objects with the value that they associate with that past. Jefferson himself would have understood this well. In 1825, the year before he died, his granddaughter Ellen lost several treasured belongings in a shipwreck—including a writing desk that had been made for her at Monticello. As a replacement, Jefferson sent her the portable desk on which he had composed the Declaration of Independence. Objects, he wrote, "acquire a superstitious value because of their connection with particular persons," and "surely a connection with the great Charter of our Independence may give a value to what has been associated with that." He joked that it might even someday be "carried in the procession of our nation's birthday as the relics of the saints are in those of the church." But Ellen's husband recognized the true value of the object: "I feel a sentiment almost of awe, and approach it with respect," he wrote. "I would fain consider it as no longer inanimate, and mute, but as something to be interrogated, and caressed."[30] We say an object is "priceless" because it is invested with this kind of spiritual value.

People also give sentimental value to property they've worked hard for. Property owners they have a right to property because they have *earned* it—they have put time, energy, labor, and worry into a house or an invention or a business. That time, energy, labor, and worry belonged, at the outset, to *them*—those things, like the food or water they have consumed, are an inalienable part of their own unique personalities. Somewhere along the line, they chose to mix *who they are*—irreplaceable, fundamental aspects of themselves, like their time, labor, and creativity—with the thing that they come to see as their "own." They tend to be especially proud of the things they have earned through hard work. The most obvious example is what lawyers call "property by creation": a person's right to own something because she made it for herself, as in the story of the Little Red Hen. When she makes the bread, the Little Red Hen thinks of it as hers, not because society or the law has given it to her, but because she went through the trouble of making it, and therefore her claim to it is more justified than the claims of the other animals, who did not create it. There are many legal and economic justifications that can also be advanced on behalf of the hen's right to own the bread, but the important thing is the moral insight that goes into declaring that she owns what she has made. We don't ask about how the laws in her jurisdiction treat property or labor—we say that the bread is hers because she has invested her time and energy in making it. That time and energy cannot be replaced or substituted. To say that the bread is "hers" is to say that she has, at some point, exchanged a part of her *self* to make it, and that depriving her of it (or of the money she might make by selling it) would be to deprive her wrongly of a part of her self.

Not only are property rights a natural aspect of individual existence, they are also universal among human societies. Although it is often claimed that some American Indian tribes had no concept of private property, that simply is not true. Native Americans had a sense of "mine" and "not-mine" and of trade[31]; in some cases, they developed sophisticated economies with long-distant trading outposts and complicated exchange agreements, all of which depended on property rights. And, just as children have been subjected to failed experiments to eradicate the concept of property, many nations have also tried to eradicate the concept of property, all without success. Even where such societies have survived for a time, they have done so at the cost of profound infringements on personal privacy and individual identity.

The importance of private property in enabling people to define their individual personalities is dramatically illustrated by the experiences of groups, such as the Shakers, that tried to abolish property. Getting their name from the way they danced and shook during worship, the Shakers established communes in several states in the 19th century; there they dedicated themselves to the principles of celibacy, sobriety, and the abolition of private property. But while

14

the Shakers were a peaceful and unusually successful movement, abolishing private property came at a high cost: their daily lives were ruthlessly cleansed of every vestige of privacy.[32] Along with the destruction of property rights came a constant war against individuality and independence. Members of the society all dressed alike, newspapers were censored, and topics of conversation had to be preapproved by elders.[33] Men and women were not allowed to visit each other without a specific reason, or pass on the stairs, or give each other gifts, or touch; in fact, they were required to keep at least five feet between them at all times. Every aspect of their routine was subject to inflexible rules, and strict enforcement was maintained by elders who spied through peepholes and from watch towers.[34] By abolishing property rights, the Shakers essentially abolished the boundaries that separated them from each other or gave them any sense of personal autonomy. Edward Andrews, a noted expert on the Shakers, concludes that "under such conditions, an atmosphere of mutual suspicion was almost inevitable; the feeling that one was being spied on every hour of the day was bound to deprive the individual of dignity and self-respect."[35] Amazingly, in spite of this relentless attack on individuality and ownership, some Shakers still managed to satisfy their desires for privacy and individuality; archaeology at Shaker villages, for example, has turned up the remains of a thriving black market in whiskey, perfume, and baldness cures.[36]

A much more horrible example of the consequences of attacking the concept of ownership was the Soviet Union's attempt to abolish private property in the 20th century. The Russian Revolution of 1917 began a catastrophe unmatched in human history, during which the Soviet government murdered some 20 million citizens and imprisoned many millions more in concentration camps.[37] The Soviet attack on private property created a nation with no safeguards against the cruelest whims of reigning dictators. The communist experiment demonstrates, better than anything ever has, how private property rights serve as a shield, protecting people against government-sponsored injustice. Shortly after the revolution put him in power, Vladimir Lenin imposed collective ownership on every business in the country that employed more than four people. The consequences were a collapse in production, famine, and economic catastrophe. Unable to enjoy the rewards of their labor, Soviet workers lost initiative; industrial production fell more than 80 percent in seven years, and grain production fell by 40 percent.[38] Lenin relented briefly, but when Stalin succeeded him, the cruel policy of collectivization resumed. In 1932, when the government ordered Ukraine's farmers to turn over an ever-increasing share of their harvest to the state, the farmers rebelled by hiding their products from government inspectors. Stalin ordered 5,400 of them executed and another 125,000 sent to prison camps.[39]

Soviet movies, books, and newspapers were censored. Artists were strictly controlled.[40] Citizens were forced to attend "spontaneous" demonstrations of loyalty to the Communist Future. Secret police watched citizens' every move, maintaining strict control over art, science, religion, education, the press, and the military, and often arresting citizens in the dark of night and subjecting them to brutal and eerily clandestine punishment. Later dictators were only slightly less cruel. Along with Nazi Germany, the Soviet experience occasioned a new word: *totalitarianism*, total government control of all aspects of life. There was no refuge for dissent or nonconformity, and few incentives for creativity. The Soviet economy was almost always stagnant; shortages and breadlines were features of daily life, and much technological advancement came from espionage or from copying Western countries. Partly because of a shortage of housing (caused by state control of the housing market), and partly because of the Soviet program to eliminate privacy, the government forced families to live together in small apartments.[41] Alcoholism became rampant—15 percent of Soviet government revenues came from the sale of alcohol alone.[42] As historian Martin Malia concludes, the heart of those great evils was the attack on property rights. "For the suppression of private property, profit, and the market is tantamount to the suppression of civil society and all individual autonomy. And although this can be approximated for a time, it requires an inordinate application of force that cannot be sustained indefinitely."[43]

Astonishingly, despite its mortifying zeal, Soviet communism never managed to create a wholly propertyless society. After the first years of communism produced famine and collapse, Lenin instituted the New Economic Plan, which sought to increase productivity by allowing producers to keep more of what they made. The NEP was shut down only a few years later, but when the Soviet government again allowed farmers to have private gardens and to keep the crops they grew there, the result was a booming black market. Meanwhile, Soviet citizens bickered jealously over even small pieces of property[44] and found ingenious ways to hide treasured belongings. Perhaps nothing better expresses the tragedy of the communist experience than the words of the novelist Ayn Rand, who escaped from the Soviet Union in the 1920s and published a novel, *We the Living*, about the country she had left behind. "Don't you know," her main character says to a Soviet soldier, "that there are things, in the best of us, which no outside hand should dare to touch? Things sacred because, and only because, one can say, 'This is *mine*'?"[45]

From the most primitive societies to the most sophisticated, from ancient history to the present day, from robust free-market societies like pre-1997 Hong Kong to the darkest tyrannies on earth, such as present-day North Korea, no society has ever existed without at least some form of private property. Even societies that have tried hard to eliminate property, and persecuted people who tried to defend it, have failed to eliminate it completely. The reason is that property rights are a natural and vital part of human existence.[46] People flourish only in societies where they can keep the things they earn and create a sphere of personal autonomy in which they can be themselves.

The Soviet Union, and many other nations that tried to abolish property rights, found their inspiration in the works of political philosophers who argued that property rights are not natural but are the product of social conventions, which can be changed. For example, Jean-Jacques Rousseau and Karl Marx (who was heavily influenced by Rousseau) contended that property is a social invention, and a basically corrupt one, which is taught to us through a sort of cultural propaganda instituted by the wealthy.[47] According to this theory, humanity originally lived in perfect harmony with nature, in a life of "noble savagery." Man in that state was supremely happy: as Allan Bloom explains, Rousseau's natural man "cannot think far into the future. He is not frightened of death because he cannot conceive it; he only avoids pain. He has no need to fight his fellow creatures except when there is a scarcity of the bare necessities."[48] Humanity fell from this Eden, however, when it developed reason and private property. Man became rational, competitive, selfish, and unequal. Those who obtained the most property then decided that the best way to protect it was to create government.

17

Government, and all the rules upon which it is founded, including the rules of private property, exists only to perpetuate that inequality. Only by overthrowing the system and creating a truly equal society—one without private property—could man once again be equal and free. In such a society, all activity would be organized by the "general will," which is not to be confused with the will of the majority or even the will of "all"; instead, the general will is the will of the "people as a whole," cleansed of selfishness by a dictator. Obeying the general will would prevent selfishness and individualism from once again creating inequality and unhappiness.

Like Rousseau, Marx and his followers speculated that, before the origin of society, human beings lived in a state of "primitive communism," in tribes that shared the product of all labor in common. Before agriculture was invented, such primitive communism allowed people to live without the problems of overpopulation and isolation. But with the invention of agriculture, a "social surplus" was created—that is, more food was created than was consumed. How to divide that surplus became a problem, and the solution was devised by the wealthier, sneakier members of the community: they invented the idea of private property, so as to monopolize as much of the surplus as possible. Property rights, therefore, are inherently connected with inequality, oppression, and exploitation of the poor.

Since the rules on which modern society is based rest on the idea of private property, Marx continues, civilization itself leads to inequality, selfishness, and poverty. The anti-social concept of "ownership" corrupts everything, including even the deepest parts of people's minds. In Marx's words, "It is not the consciousness of men that determines their being, but, on the contrary, their social being that determines their consciousness."[49] And since the existence of property rights "determines the consciousness" of everyone in society, no transaction can *really* be the product of a free agreement, even though the people involved may think it is. An employee, for instance, may think he is freely choosing to work for an employer, but in reality he is being exploited and robbed of his freedom. He is controlled, subtly, by the wealthy manipulators of society, through the very idea of ownership. To make people *really* free, therefore, we must abolish private property and build a society in which individual acts are organized by "society as a whole."

There are several flaws with such theories, not the least of which is the fact that they are not supported by history. There is no evidence that humans ever lived in any state of "primitive communism." Private property is a natural part of the way humans live and flourish. Moreover, private property, and especially the private ownership of "surplus" capital, is enormously beneficial to society—particularly to those who are least well off—because those who own surplus capital can invest it in experimental new enterprises that raise the standard of living and create jobs. Those innovations make every hour of labor more productive, which gives rise to more food, more goods, and even more leisure time.

Worst of all, however, Rousseau's and Marx's theories are profoundly hostile to individual initiative and even to the notion that individuals can think for themselves. This makes room for dangerous levels of control by government. If people's minds are made up for them by the "relations of production" that are "independent of their will," then there is little room for important spiritual values like independence, integrity, or self-determination. The terrible crimes that communist societies have committed against people are the direct consequence of Marx's rejection of individualism. In Marxist societies, individuals are generally considered expendable—tools that government may use in the name of the "public good." Because the "public" is virtually impossible to identify and what is "good" for it is always open to debate, such a perspective allows government to get away with doing almost anything, no matter how cruel.

The idea of property rights originates, not with social agreement, but with individuals who deserve to keep the things they earn and to use the things that belong to them. There is no basis for the belief that property is created by society or government. Yet that belief is still widely espoused by political and legal intellectuals. For example, law professor Cass Sunstein has argued that "governmental rules lie behind the exercise of rights of property, contract, and tort," so that a regime of private property is itself simply a creation of the state; thus the state may change the rules—depriving people of what they absurdly suppose are "their" things—whenever doing so is in society's interest. "A major problem with the pre–New Deal framework," he writes,

> was that it treated the existing distribution of resources and opportunities as prepolitical and presocial . . . when in fact it was not. . . . [The] private or voluntary private sphere . . . was actually itself a creation of law and hardly purely voluntary. When the law of trespass enabled an employer to

> exclude an employee from "his" property unless the
> employee met certain conditions, the law was crucially
> involved. Without the law of trespass, and accompanying
> legal rules of contract and tort, the relationship between
> employers and employees would not be what it now is;
> indeed, it would be extremely difficult to figure out what
> that relationship might be, if it would exist in recognizable
> form at all.[50]

Played out to its logical conclusion, Sunstein's argument means that when a burglar breaks into a person's house, that person's feelings of humiliation and fear exist only because our society has declared that burglary is illegal—not because the victim's personal rights have been violated. Society could just declare that burglary will now be permitted, and then the victims would not feel violated.

It's certainly true that without the law of trespass, relationships between people would be different. But Sunstein does not elaborate on what such a society might really be like, or on the more important question of whether such a society would be one in which people would flourish. Would people be happy in a society that allowed burglary? Interestingly, Sunstein fails to discuss why, in his example, an employer or a homeowner might *want* to exclude other people from what Sunstein calls "his" (in quotes) property. The obvious answer is because an employer or a homeowner considers the property to be his *own*, not merely because the *law* says so, but for a deeper reason. The owner sees the law only as supporting a claim that is based on the more fundamental principle of his right to the fruits of his labor. Is he justified in feeling that way? Or is his desire to exclude based only on the state having given him permission to do so by granting him a property right?

As all the failed attempts to abolish private property show, people have a natural yearning for property; they have a natural desire for self-definition and autonomy that expresses itself through private property—even when they are relentlessly indoctrinated in an attempt to purge the idea from them. Societies that weaken protections of property rights cause great suffering and distress to those who desire privacy, who want to express themselves, or who want to keep the fruits of their labor. Property is not a politically created institution that can be manipulated at will. It is a natural aspect of our humanity.

Property Is Good for Individuals

Frederick Douglass was born a slave. A terrible exception to the Declaration of Independence's assertion that "all men are created equal," slavery was based on the notion that some people are entitled to exercise power over others without their consent—in fact, to own them as property. Douglass recalled bitterly how it felt on the days when his master sent him to work in the shipyards of Baltimore and then forced him to hand over the wages the shipyard had paid him. "I began to show signs of disquiet with slavery," he says.

> I was living among *freemen*, and was in all respects equal to them by nature and attainments. *Why should I be a slave?* There was *no* reason why I should be the thrall of any man. Besides, I was now getting, as I have said, a dollar and fifty cents per day. I contracted for it, worked for it, collected it; it was paid to me, and it was *rightfully* my own; and yet upon every returning Saturday night, this money—my own hard earnings, every cent of it—was demanded of me and taken from me by Master Hugh. He did not earn it; he had no hand in earning it; why, then, should he have it?[51]

Douglass believed that he owned himself and his labor. If he chose to use that labor by exchanging it for money from an employer, he, not Master Hugh, had the right to the wages he received in exchange. In short, Douglass believed that all men are created equal. That does not mean that all people are exactly alike, but simply that no person is naturally entitled to use force on another person in the same way that, for instance, a human uses a hammer to drive a nail.[52] As Thomas Jefferson put it, 50 years after writing the Declaration, "[T]he mass of mankind has not been born with saddles on their backs, nor a favored few booted and spurred, ready to ride them legitimately, by the grace of God."[53]

Shortly after starting work at the shipyards, Douglass began to plan his escape. Disguising himself as a sailor, and using a forged Navy pass, he fled to New York, where he was taken in by agents of the Underground Railroad. Once he was free, Douglass had to find a way to support himself, so he began to look for work. He described how different he felt about work after his escape:

> On my way down Union street I saw a large pile of coal in front of the house of Rev. Ephraim Peabody, the Unitarian minister. I went to the kitchen door and asked the privilege

> of bringing in and putting away this coal. "What will you charge?" said the lady. "I will leave that to you, madam." "You may put it away," she said. I was not long in accomplishing the job, when the dear lady put into my hand *two silver half dollars*. To understand the emotion which swelled my heart as I clasped this money, realizing that I had no master who could take it from me—*that it was mine*—*that my hands were my own*, and could earn more of the precious coin—one must have been in some sense himself a slave.[54]

Douglass had discovered the essential meaning of property rights. Property is the practical way of implementing the idea of self-ownership. For Master Hugh to take his earnings away meant that Hugh had the right to take away his labor, which means his body and his liberty, against his will. As Abraham Lincoln put it, slavery was simply "the same old serpent that says you work and I eat, you toil and I will enjoy the fruits of it."[55]

Almost two centuries before Douglass escaped from slavery, the English political philosopher John Locke had explained the principle of self-ownership in his *Second Treatise of Civil Government*. God had created man and then put each person in control of his or her own destiny, within certain natural boundaries. "Every man has a *property* in his own *person*," he wrote. "This nobody has any right to but himself. The *labor* of his body, and the *work* of his hands, we may say, are properly his."[56] For someone else—or for a group of people—to deprive a person of the product of his labor would be, so to speak, stealing that person from himself and from God. The legislature "is not, nor can possibly be, absolutely arbitrary over the lives and fortunes of the people," because it only has "the joint power of every member of the society."[57] And since nobody can have the right to deprive another person of what he or she has earned, nobody can transfer such authority to the government. Each person is in charge of his own life and the fruits of his labor; the government exists simply to ensure that people respect each other's rights.

Property rights thus build a sphere of privacy around a person, within which he or she is free to act without anyone else interfering: a realm of personal dominion where people may make their own choices. Property rights minimize the degree to which people may use *force* against each other and require them to deal with one another on the basis of mutual respect, deliberation, and cooperation. This increases their freedom. The connection between property and self-determination is best summarized in the famous feminist slogan from Virginia Woolf: "a room of my own." A realm of individual choice and privacy depends on the fact that the room is *her own* and that no other person may intrude there against her will.

One reason people desire privacy is because they are different. People often seek places where they can "be themselves" without worrying about what others might think. This desire for privacy often leads people to set boundaries between themselves and the rest of the world so that they can commune with themselves—to look inward, to think, and to appreciate life. Perhaps no writer has better expressed these desires than Henry David Thoreau, the author of *Walden*, who described his decision to move away from the city to the countryside, where he could be apart from the world. Among "the real attractions" of life at Walden Pond, he wrote, were "its complete retirement, being, about two miles from the village, half a mile from the nearest neighbor, and separated from the highway by a broad field . . . and the dilapidated fences, which put such an interval between me and the last occupant."[58] The farm was a place where Thoreau felt he could face life directly without having it "frittered away by detail" in confrontation with bustling society. Reflecting on the connection between property and privacy, Thoreau quoted from the poet William Cowper: "I am monarch of all I survey, / My right there is none to dispute."

People not only protect their privacy with houses and land; they also use their personal possessions to give them a sense of independence and boundaries. People often put up photographs or postcards in their offices, for example, or keep souvenirs of vacations. These things enable people to reflect on what is important to them and to take a brief respite from the world. Without such belongings, people would be less able to block out things that they might not want to worry about. Another example is portable music devices. Commenting recently on the development of personal listening technologies, Nancy Friedrich, editor of *Wireless Systems Design* magazine, recalled how she felt when she got her first Walkman. "That Walkman ranks up there as one of my favorite gifts of all time," she wrote. "I even remember the first cassette that I played in it. To me, that Walkman represented freedom. I could listen to music without waking my little sister. I also gained some much-needed privacy. With the Walkman, it was harder for my older brother and sister to criticize my playlist. Plus, my parents didn't have to tell me to turn it down."[59] A small piece of personal property gave her a sense of independence and self-determination that she cherished.

Of course, that very fact led some to criticize the Walkman. "The social pleasure of sharing music was terminated when people clamped plugs in their ears and tuned into a selfish sound," writes music critic Norman Lebrecht.[60] "Music in the Walkman era ceased to connect us one to another. It promoted autism and isolation, with consequences yet untold." But what young Nancy enjoyed most about her Walkman was precisely that it allowed her to *escape* having to "share" music that she didn't enjoy, and to "selfishly" choose her own music instead. Even Lebrecht recognizes the importance of such personal autonomy when he fondly recalls using a Walkman to listen to "Mahler's Resurrection Symphony on a vertical Alpine train as a thunderstorm crashed all around. In unforgettable settings, music acquired unsuspected dimensions." Presumably Lebrecht would not have had the same pleasure had he been forced to listen to someone else's musical choice of, say, Chuck Berry's "My Dingaling."

People not only use land and personal property to differentiate themselves from other people and to express themselves individually; they also use their property to express themselves in groups that share their values with others. Edward J. Bloustein, an expert on the law of privacy rights, called this "the right to huddle."[61] Whether it be an antique car club, or a political party, or a sports team, or a church, people use private property to "huddle" together and share their interests. Religious groups in particular use property to bring people together and pursue a common mission. A church serves as a refuge, a meeting place, and an important source of personal identity for its congregation. The concept of "fellowship" is profoundly important to religious groups,[62] and spreading the word is an integral part of many people's faith.

The Cottonwood Christian Center of Orange County, California, put a very heavy emphasis on the importance of raising Christian awareness. "The teachings of Jesus," explained Cottonwood's senior pastor Bayless Conley, required his congregation "to make a lasting impact in the Orange and Los Angeles County communities . . . by ministering to the spiritual and physical needs of the members of these communities."[63] Cottonwood's members put their hearts into it, and from 50 founding members in 1983, their church grew to more than 5,000 members in 2002. Cottonwood ran a television ministry and offered six worship services every weekend to accommodate the large crowds. But the center's facilities were outdated and could seat only 700 attendees at any one time. Cottonwood needed a new building. "The Bible teaches all individual Christians to join a church," explained Pastor Conley. "Because the church is one body, it is essential to our faith that the whole church body regularly assemble together as a body to worship God's divine ordinances."[64]

Cottonwood decided to build a new church with seating for 4,700 people, classrooms, study areas, a daycare center, and even a gymnasium. In 1999 it bought 18 acres in the city of Cypress. But city officials had other plans. They had long wanted to see a shopping center built on the site, and although most of the city's "redevelopment project area" was still languishing vacant after almost 15 years, the city rejected Cottonwood's application for a building permit and immediately issued a moratorium on all construction in the area. The moratorium stayed in place for two years while officials drafted a plan for an open-air shopping mall that would include restaurants and movie theaters. When developers showed little interest, the city adopted another new plan. Under this plan, they would transform 18 acres of land into a retail shopping center—the same 18 acres that just happened to be owned by Cottonwood. This time the city had a retailer in mind: Costco, which proposed building a 150,000-square foot warehouse store on the site. In May 2002 the city condemned Cottonwood's property. The church filed a lawsuit in federal court, arguing—just as Susette Kelo would later argue in her case—that the condemnation was not for a "public use" but for Costco's private use instead.

Judge David O. Carter ruled in favor of Cottonwood. The city, he wrote, had done nothing with the property for more than a decade, while "Cottonwood spent a year assembling the property without any government help."[65] It was only after Cottonwood asked the city to approve its expansion plans that the city "moved aggressively to find other uses for the property."[66] The government's last-minute plan to shift the property to a more profitable retail use was a serious violation of Cottonwood's property rights and a major obstacle to its religious mission. "Once it is stripped of the ownership

25

of the land," Judge Carter noted, "Cottonwood will have to start from square one. Although the City blithely asserts that Cottonwood can buy some other property . . . it took Cottonwood four years to identify the appropriate location to build a church, and another year of negotiations to acquire the separate parcels." If the condemnation were permitted, Cottonwood would have to "wedge its growing congregation into ill-suited facilities for another five years."[67] But Carter held that Cottonwood could keep its land.

Cottonwood and other churches use property to bring people together in what lawyers call "expressive association." This kind of association develops a community of ideas and allows people to express themselves in company with others.[68] When property rights are not secure, churches and other groups cannot accomplish that mission, which harms the ability of individuals to express themselves and follow their beliefs.

Expressive association also requires that people be able to set themselves apart from those who do not share their values or who might even despise them. Theologian Paul Tillich argued that faith is only meaningful in the context of a shared community, because a shared vocabulary of tradition, symbol, and myth is an integral part of religious identity, and these can have no meaning in isolation.[69] But coming together to share a faith is possible only when the church serves as a refuge from those who oppose it. A church therefore "excludes from its community those who are thought to have denied the foundations of the church."[70] Although Tillich believed that a church should tolerate some differences of opinion, he insisted that it must also defend the integrity of its core beliefs. Without the ability to draw boundaries between the congregation and the rest of the world, its identity will be diluted and its mission compromised.[71] Private property is one of the most important tools for maintaining those boundaries.

In 2001 the Church of Christ in Hollywood faced a serious problem when one of its members, a woman named Lady Cage-Barile, grew angry at the way the church was being run.[72] In particular, she complained that the minister and several churchgoers had divorced and remarried, which she believed violated biblical principles. Ignoring the minister's request that she find another church, she disrupted Bible study and harassed church members, shouting at them that they were demons and agents of Satan destined for punishment and eternal damnation. The church's youth group became so concerned about her behavior that they began meeting in secret. In 2002 the congregation voted to expel her, but she still kept coming, shouting during services, calling people names, and tearing posters off the walls. The minister asked a Los Angeles court to issue a restraining order against her, but the judge refused. This was an internal church affair, he said, and a restraining order would violate her freedom of speech.[73] But the appellate court overruled that decision. Churches have the right "to define themselves and their religious message," and that includes the right to bar people who disrupt their services and denigrate their values.[74] "Simply put," the court concluded, "Cage-Barile is a trespasser. The pertinent question, then, is whether a church or religious organization can exclude unwelcome persons from its premises. The answer is yes."[75] Having a place apart from those who despise our beliefs and our lifestyles is essential to creating and maintaining any group identity. Just as the Democratic Party must be free to exclude Republicans from its ranks,[76] religious groups and civic organizations must have the right to create an identity for themselves by excluding those who disagree with them.

In short, whether people choose to join together with others who share their values or to seclude themselves in a modern-day Walden, property allows people to be different—to *dissent*. Individually, or in groups, people use property to draw boundaries between themselves and the world, boundaries that allow them not only to define themselves in opposition to those they disagree with but also to create a personal identity with their property: their homes, their personal belongings, and especially their "sentimental" property. William Blackstone, the 18th-century English lawyer, recognized that property rights were essentially a way for people to preserve their right to be different. He explained that individual rights

> may be reduced to three principal or primary articles; the right of personal security, the right of personal liberty, and the right of private property: because, as there is no other known method of compulsion, or of abridging man's natural free will, but by an infringement or diminution of one or other of these important rights.[77]

Not only do we define ourselves in relation to our homes and churches; we define ourselves in relation to our work as well. Many owners of small businesses, in particular, treasure the feeling of independence and self-sufficiency that they get from operating their own stores or restaurants. James Chan was born in China in 1949 and was working for a large New York corporation in the early 1980s when he decided to go into business for himself. He was on a business trip in Florida, scoping out the company's new headquarters, when the thought struck him that he simply was not happy with his job. "I was going to move to a place I didn't like to work for a boss I didn't respect, devoting my energies to office politics for which I had little talent," he recalls thinking. "I was going to make this sacrifice so that I could afford the surf and turf at an elaborately mediocre restaurant on the outskirts of nowhere. . . . This was my life, and I was getting set to waste it."[78] Deciding he would rather be his own boss, Chan started Asia Marketing and Management, a consulting firm that advises American companies on doing business in China. "It has been 17 years since that night," he writes. "I am free. I feel free. I own myself."[79]

For Chan, the feeling of self-reliance and self-direction is the most important benefit of running his own business—far more important than financial success. The reward of working for oneself "comes in personal satisfaction, in autonomy, in deliverance from office politics, in the freedom to make [one's] own mistakes instead of being forced to execute the misjudgments of others. Living by your wits can be risky, but it also makes you feel more alive."[80] That is why Chan calls himself a "tycoon," a word that "comes, as I do, from China. It refers to one who rules, a sovereign. . . . My empire is small, but I do rule it. And I'd rather be captain of my dinghy than a junior officer on the *Titanic*."[81]

That sense of economic independence may be the best definition of "the American dream," and over the years it has attracted countless immigrants, like Chan, to the United States. When Ahmad Mesdaq fled the Soviet invasion of his homeland, Afghanistan, he hoped to start a new, secure life in the United States, where he could earn an honest living for himself and his family. Mesdaq opened a cigar store in the Gaslamp District of San Diego in 1994. The Gran Havana Cigar Factory, as he called it, sold not only fine cigars, but fancy coffee as well, to upper-middle-class residents and tourists who enjoyed the Gaslamp District's old-town setting.

But years before he bought the property, city officials had declared the neighborhood "blighted," meaning that the area's businesses were not performing up to the standard that bureaucrats desired. California's vague legal definition of "blight" meant that there was little the area's landowners could do, and, worse, state law severely restricted their opportunities for a day in court. In 2005, when the city finally condemned his store, the area was far from blighted— in fact, it was quite fashionable, and the Gran Havana Cigar Factory was pleased to host such upscale cigar aficionados as California governor Arnold Schwarzenegger. Nevertheless, the city moved forward with its plans to condemn the shop and give the land to a developer to build a hotel.

Mesdaq filed a lawsuit, but the trial court held that California law did not allow him to introduce any new evidence to show that the blight designation was wrong. When he appealed, the city explained to the court that if the condemnation did not go forward, "the number of rooms [would be] reduced from 334 rooms to 237," the "on-site parking [would be] reduced," the hotel would lose "150 linear feet of street footage," and the size of the ballroom and lobby areas would have to be reduced.[82] The court of appeal ruled in favor of the city, and the state supreme court refused to take the case. On June 13, 2005, Mesdaq closed his store for the last time. "All I wanted to do was live the American dream," he reflected. "Is that too much to ask?"[83]

Mesdaq, like Chan, sought to define and express himself through his work. Private property rights ought to preserve that freedom of choice and the fruits of one's labor. When the government ignores or violates those rights, it endangers the well-being not only of individual citizens but of society in general. There is little incentive to invest in a community and work to improve it if the government can take property away at any time and give it to some other person or group that the bureaucrats prefer.

Not only does private property allow individuals to define themselves and come together with others who share their values, it also allows them to plan for the future, to secure their retirement or insure against possible future losses. Since every life has its ups and downs, people must take care to provide for emergencies and bad times. When people can rely on the security of their private property rights, they can make plans for the future. People buy homes, land, stocks, bonds, gold, art, antiques, and other things not only for enjoyment but also to save their money. They can, in essence, store the value of their labor indefinitely and use it at a later date. That enables people to set long-term goals by putting aside enough money to fix up their homes, to open a business, to marry and have children, to send their children to college, or to prepare a comfortable retirement. But when government infringes on their right to property, people are less free to plan for the future or to insure against future calamities. Unfortunately, the elderly often learn only at the last minute that the dreams they've pursued for years can be overridden by government in the blink of an eye.

John and Carol Pappas were Greek immigrants who arrived in the United States in the 1940s. They moved to the Las Vegas area where John bought 7,000 square feet of land, including a small shopping center. The Pappases leased the land out to support themselves, and John would often tell his wife, "When I die, you'll have this property to support you. . . . This is going to be your retirement."[84] But in 1985 the city council created a redevelopment agency with the idea of redesigning the city's downtown. Even though there was no evidence that the Pappases' property was blighted in any way, the city adopted a redevelopment plan that involved the condemnation of several Las Vegas properties, including the Pappases'.

The next year, when the Pappases and other landowners became concerned that the plan might involve eminent domain, the city held a public hearing—a hearing that a judge later described as a sham. "City officials," the judge wrote, "repeatedly assured the citizenry that eminent domain would rarely be used."[85] The mayor told the audience that the government was not going to "wipe out all of Downtown Las Vegas including your area into a big empty lot and then start building."[86] The city attorney agreed: "I think people may be getting upset about something that really is never going to happen."[87] And a city councilman joined in: "I'd just like to make one comment about eminent domain. This Board has always had the power of eminent [domain]—and you've seen how we use it in the past. Never . . . since I've been on this Board."[88] Citizens who continued to express doubts were shushed, or ignored outright:

> [I]n the exchange between Mayor Briare and a Mrs. Clark
> . . . Mrs. Clark seeks to learn if any of the comments at the
> hearing will change anything in the text [of the redevelop-
> ment plan]. Briare informs her that the board will decide the
> question. Mrs. Clark persists and asks what sections in the

Plan protect an individual citizen. Briare tells her that the protection is this public hearing. He cuts her off without answering her question by stating that there is "nothing in here that is designed to hurt them."[89]

Those assurances that their property would be safe lured the property owners into not challenging the legality of the city's plan.

In 1993 a group of casinos decided to construct an open-air pedestrian mall including casinos, retail outlets, and topless bars, called Fremont Street Experience. They created a corporation to handle the construction. Because the Experience needed a parking garage, the corporation executed an agreement with the Las Vegas Redevelopment Agency whereby the agency would condemn the Pappas family's land and transfer it to the corporation. On November 19, 1993, the city filed its eminent domain case, but it did not serve the Pappases with papers for another three weeks. At the same time that it filed the case, though, the city also asked the court for an expedited procedure—of which the Pappases were not notified. As a later court put it, "What the Pappas Family had owned for nearly fifty years was stripped from them in less than 50 seconds in a summary proceeding . . . at which they were not even present."[90] When the Pappases' attorney found out about the dirty dealings, he asked the court for reconsideration, but the judge said no. The Pappases filed a new lawsuit—now that their property had been taken from them—but after years of litigation, they lost their case. Today, the Pappas family's land is a parking garage.

John Pappas's faith that his property would help take care of his wife after he died was demolished along with his property. When property rights are not respected, even the most careful plans for the future can be obliterated whenever the government chooses.

Property Is Good for Society

Private property isn't just good for individuals; it is essential to a safe, prosperous, and happy society as well.

For centuries, political philosophers and economists have studied the ways people interact with property. More than two thousand years ago, Plato argued that property rights foster selfishness and individualism, which he claimed are destructive to society. Property should be abolished among a country's rulers, he wrote, so that they will concentrate solely on public concerns.[91] In fact, the ideal society would be one that had "eliminate[d] everything we mean by the word *ownership* from life." Banning ownership would make the whole society act as if it were one person, and all people would "see, hear, act, in the common service."[92]

Aristotle disagreed. There might be cases of people developing an unhealthy fixation on property, he said, but for the most part property was an inherent part of human life, and a healthy one. Secure property rights mean that people "will not complain of one another, and they will make more progress, because everyone will be attending to his own business."[93] A society in which everyone acts the same is not necessarily desirable, Aristotle wrote, and it was silly to imagine that by abolishing property, "in some wonderful manner everybody will become everybody's friend."[94] There will always be jealousy and bickering in every society—but where property rights are protected, people are required to respect each others' boundaries. As the poet Robert Frost put it, "Good fences make good neighbors."[95] Nobel laureate Friedrich Hayek explained:

> The understanding that "good fences make good neigh-
> bours," that is, that men can use their own knowledge in
> the pursuit of their own ends without colliding with each
> other only if clear boundaries can be drawn between their
> respective domains of free action, is the basis on which all
> known civilization has grown. Property . . . is the only solu-
> tion men have yet discovered to the problem of reconciling
> individual freedom with an absence of conflict. . . . There can
> be no law in the sense of universal rules of conduct which
> does not determine boundaries of the domains of freedom
> by laying down rules that enable each to ascertain where he
> is free to act.[96]

Secure property rights allow people to differ, while still remaining polite and even friendly. That's why Tom Bethell, in his history of property rights, *The Noblest Triumph,* describes property as "the most peaceable of institutions."[97] On Election Day, Americans with the most profound disagreements settle their disputes peacefully at the ballot box and then return to their homes, unafraid of reprisals or recriminations if their favored candidate should lose. The "good fences" principle—or the "live and let live" principle—serves as a foundation for a healthy society. To put it another way, toleration is the key to polite deliberation. Parents often introduce their children to this idea at an early age, when they teach them that getting along with others requires them to respect each other's boundaries. In fact, the *Parents' Answer Book* advises parents that "children have a strong need for stability and security. They need to know that some things are theirs and theirs alone and that their needs are just as important as another child's needs."[98] Why should we suppose that things are any different for adults?

When property rights break down and people face the possibility of losing their homes or businesses at the conclusion of a political campaign, the social bonds that make for healthy communities break down also. A particularly sad example of that occurred in the early 1980s, when officials in Detroit, Michigan, condemned an entire working-class neighborhood, called "Poletown" because of the large number of Polish immigrants who lived there, to make way for a car factory. A severe recession had boosted the state's unemployment rate to 12.2 percent and lowered the city's tax base by $100 million[99] when General Motors announced that it was considering locations for a new plant. Using mostly federal grant money,[100] the city condemned hundreds of homes and businesses, evicted 4,200 residents, and demolished the 465-acre neighborhood to transfer the property to General Motors.

Controversy over the project turned what was once a peaceful, integrated community into a battleground. At first, people opposed to the condemnation set up picket lines in front of public buildings,[101] but after the Michigan Supreme Court upheld the condemnation as valid under the state's "public use" clause,[102] formerly polite neighbors became angry and fearful. One group of homeowners protested by driving a bulldozer onto the lawn of GM president Roger Smith on Mother's Day and covering it with signs reading "Happy Mother's Day, Mrs. Smith, Talk To Roger."[103] Two Poletown residents were arrested for trying to burn down the offices of a GM contractor.[104] When GM held its annual stockholders' meeting, protesters repeatedly tried to seize the microphone; the company's executives spoke behind a bulletproof podium, and slipped in and out of the meeting through a secure underground tunnel. Civility was one of the casualties of the *Poletown* case, concludes writer Jean Wylie. "People whose lives were composed of their union loyalty, their tenure in the auto plants, their patriotism, and their willingness to fight in U.S. wars were rejected, ignored, and robbed by the very institutions through which they claimed their identities."[105] The incident remained a subject of controversy for decades afterward. Then, in another eminent domain case decided in August 2004, the Michigan Supreme Court admitted that its decision to allow the Poletown condemnation had been wrong. It overruled the prior decision—but too late for those who had long since lost their homes and businesses.

A healthy society rests on civility and respect. Civility and respect, in turn, depend on people being able to trust that their rights will be honored. That is why societies with greater degrees of tolerance tend to feature more community involvement.[106]

In addition, as Aristotle recognized, private property is more effective in ensuring society's prosperity because property that is not owned by anyone "has the least amount of care bestowed upon it."[107] Economists call this the "tragedy of the commons": when property is not owned by anyone in particular, or when people using property do not have to pay for the damage they do to it, nobody will take responsibility for the costs of maintaining it. People litter public highways, or write graffiti on freeway overpasses, or leave it to their coworkers to wash the dishes in the office kitchen because others lack the incentive to prevent such abuses. But when property is privately owned, the owner has incentives to protect and improve it. Environmental problems are often a result of the tragedy of the commons. When land is unowned, or is owned by some abstract "public," people using that property have less reason to preserve it; they may as well exploit it to satisfy their momentary desires. On the other hand, when property is privately owned, the owner and his guests are more likely to practice wise stewardship and protect it for the future.

As Bethell puts it, "Property sets up fences, but it also surrounds us with mirrors, reflecting back upon us the consequences of our own behavior."[108] Private property requires owners to bear the costs of their own activities, which means that they must take responsibility for what they do. Privately owned homes are typically far better maintained than public housing projects or college dormitories, because any decrease in the property's value must be borne by the owner and any increase in its value benefits the owner. Economists call the costs that a person imposes on another "negative externalities" because those costs are "external" to the property owner. Pollution is an "externality" because a person can pollute a river and not have to suffer the consequences. Property rights, however, help to "internalize" externalities, by requiring people to pay for any damage they inflict on another's property. Where property rights are weakly enforced, or where there is no clear owner who can prevent damage to a piece of property, people can get away with polluting, because the victims are not in a position to demand compensation.

Civility and social responsibility depend on private property rights. Economic prosperity depends on them as well. Private property allows for the most important economic activity of all: assembling capital. Entrepreneurs must have more than just ideas for new products or businesses. Since new ideas are always risky, innovators need to start out with money in hand; as the old saying has it, you have to have money to make money. Some entrepreneurs mortgage their homes to raise the capital to start a business. Others borrow from friends and family or from a bank. But in any case, property is the essential spark that starts the engine of ingenuity and wealth creation.

The Peruvian economist Hernando de Soto recently investigated several societies to see how difficult it was to start new businesses. He concluded that while many Third World countries have the resources necessary to start businesses and raise the standard of living, they lack the legal structures necessary for bringing that capital together in a form entrepreneurs can use. "Any asset whose economic and social aspects are not fixed in a formal property system is extremely hard to move in the market," he explains.[109] A system of documents, such as land titles and contracts, as well as a legal system that predictably enforces property rights, serves as a kind of engine that transforms tangible assets into useful capital. Without such a formal property rights system, tangible assets will be "like water in a lake high in the Andes—an untapped stock of potential energy."[110]

De Soto explains that systems of property law have six features that enable entrepreneurs to transform the objects they possess into the sort of start-up capital that they need to get new businesses operating and get on their way to improving their living standards.

First, property rights allow people to describe the things they have in a formal way—the way a deed describes a plot of land on a single piece of paper. Second, a formal legal property system allows all property, of whatever type—cars, jewelry, houses, livestock—to be integrated into a single, unified legal framework. When assets are left out of the legal system—for example, illegally owned objects—they can't be used to generate capital or credit. Third, a system of property rules ensures that people are accountable for the way they use their property. This permits people who have been injured by a property owner to seek redress, and it ensures that people who use their property wisely can reap the rewards. Fourth, property rules make property values fungible: they allow values in different kinds of property to be treated the same way, so that they can be compared and converted. While the value of, say, a herd of cattle might be quite high, there are many people who have no use for a herd of cattle. Formal property rules allow the value of the cattle to be transformed, first into a piece of paper and then into another kind of property—say, a car—for which another person might have a use. By letting people transform their property and divide or combine it in new and different ways, property rules allow people to make more choices about how to spend their time and resources. The fifth effect of property rights rules is to bring people into a vast network with one another: the rules allow borrowers and lenders, sellers and buyers, inventors and marketers, employers and employees to coordinate their different talents in ways that they might not otherwise have imagined. Finally, systems of property rights ensure that transactions are protected. Since so much of human life consists of avoiding the loss of what we have, property rights systems serve our needs by providing legal security to our homes, businesses, cars, televisions, stereos, jewelry, photos—to all kinds of property. In a well-developed property rights system, extremely complicated transactions can be processed in an instant, with little risk to the parties to the transaction.[111]

Perhaps the most obvious way that private property is good for society is that it creates profit incentives. People work or start their own businesses hoping to make a living for themselves and their families. As Adam Smith explained, "[I]t is not from the benevolence of the butcher, the brewer, or the baker, that we expect our dinner, but from their regard to their own interest."[112] It is people's natural desire for the things that make their lives easier and happier that drives them to work hard and to create. They know that they can exchange their labor or their creations for the products and services they need. Critics of property rights often label this motivation

36

"greed" or "selfishness," but in fact there is nothing wrong with this kind of selfishness. It is one of the most basic ingredients of virtue and hard work, and in a society that respects property rights, people will tend to be led by this healthy self-interest to produce things that other people want and to engage in peaceful exchange. Ahmad Mesdaq's desire to make a success of his cigar store and the Pappas family's desire to keep the land they counted on for their retirement income were "selfish" in the sense that Mesdaq and the Pappases wanted those things for themselves and did not want to give them up to others. That's the sort of selfishness that makes for a happy, healthy society. People have a natural need for personal identity and individual integrity. Selfishness is wrong only when it leads people to harm others—to violate their neighbors' rights to their own property and privacy. And it is in preventing and punishing that *perverse* sort of selfishness that property rights do their greatest good. In short, property rights allow people to "selfishly" pursue their own dreams—while restraining harmful expressions of selfishness by requiring them to respect everyone else's right to do the same.

Of course, private property also fosters a sense of civility, respect, and benevolence that underlies healthy charity. When people are free to make their own choices, they will often feel a greater willingness to contribute to others who are in need. By contrast, people will tend to grow resentful when they are forced to give up their earnings to others—as Frederick Douglass discovered—for forced "charity" tends to breed bitterness rather than good will. Moreover, when people are forced to be charitable, they can hardly be praised for their generosity. It is only when people freely decide to give that we feel gratitude or admiration for them.

By rewarding people for their hard work, private property rights create incentives for people to exchange those rights in productive pursuits that ultimately benefit society in general. And the exchange of property rights combines incentives with information in ways that coordinate the behavior of people who don't know each other. That is accomplished through the mechanism of prices, which transmit information in a form that carries with it the incentive to act upon it. A rising price tells consumers to be more "economical" in their use of a good, and it tells producers to make more of it. Producing the most with a given amount of resources requires that we know the cheapest way to produce a product. By giving us the knowledge we need to compare costs and benefits of different options, prices serve as a simple, effective way for people to make choices about what materials to use and what products and services to create. Those choices, in turn, are influenced by the needs of everyone else in society. The result is a more efficient organization of society, which still respects individual freedom.[113]

The economist Ludwig von Mises gave a memorable example:[114] Suppose a company is trying to build a railroad between two cities, and it comes to a mountain. Now the company must decide whether to build the railroad around the mountain, or over the mountain, or perhaps to blast a tunnel through the mountain. By comparing the relative prices of the labor and materials that each option would require, the company can choose what to do. But the prices will be set by the supply of and demand for those things among the rest of the people in society. Thus, if dynamite, for example, is needed for some other project, then the price of dynamite will go up—making the tunnel option more expensive. The railroad's owners might therefore choose to go around the mountain, because "society prefers" that the dynamite be used for another project.

Prices convey information about scarcity and social needs, which tells people how they should use and conserve their resources. Prices deter waste and encourage people to economize, and this process depends entirely on the security of private property rights. Where the government can control the prices of goods and services, or take property away from some people and give it to others, it becomes harder for people to compare the costs and benefits of different plans. "In the face of the ordinary, everyday problems which the management of an economy presents," Mises concluded, a society without property rights "would stand helpless, for it would have no possible way of keeping its accounts."[115] In fact, this problem of "economic calculation" did occur in communist societies. After the Berlin Wall came down, it was revealed that East German stores had been unable to figure out what prices to put on appliances, so they had simply copied the prices charged by Western stores.[116]

Whether it be a major industrial undertaking such as constructing a railroad, or personal goals such as saving for retirement, or budgeting the family grocery bill, sensible decisionmaking depends on the security of private property rights.

What Would Society Be Like without Property?

John Lennon once urged us to "imagine no possessions." He was right that it isn't hard to do, but when we think realistically about what such a society would actually be like, the image is a lot less pleasant than Lennon supposed.

First, a world with no possessions would suffer from social ills almost beyond imagining. Many opponents of property rights imagine that citizens can be trained to avoid conflicts even without the boundaries that are set by private property, but experience has shown the opposite. Even in societies that curtail ownership, people still have desires and disagreements. Without the good fences that make good neighbors, people would be able to take things from each other whenever they wanted. Stronger people could take things away from weaker people; majorities could dispossess minorities; unpopular people, religious dissenters, and nonconformists could suffer retaliation and persecution at any moment. Respect for differences would erode, and unpopular groups would suffer.

Unfortunately, we know from history how racial minorities suffer through the violation of their property rights. When the Nazis came to power in Germany in the 1930s, one of their first goals was to confiscate property owned by Jews.[117] And despite its rhetoric of "equality" and "brotherhood," the Soviet Union, which also confiscated property, was no haven for racial unity.[118]

In 1879 my home state of California adopted a new constitution aimed at excluding Chinese immigrants. Nativists complained that the Chinese were "taking jobs" away from white workers and that they worked so hard and were so intelligent that no American or European could hope to compete with them. Led by the cry, "The Chinese Must Go!" the Workingmen's Party called a constitutional convention where they narrowly failed to include a section forbidding the Chinese from owning any property in the state.[119] Although that provision did not pass, California legislators found other ways of forbidding Chinese and Japanese immigrants from owning land. First, western politicians managed to ban all immigration from China in the 1880s. Then in 1913 the state passed the Alien Land Act,[120] forbidding any person who was "ineligible for citizenship"—meaning the Chinese and Japanese—from owning land or leasing it for more than three years.[121]

In the 40 years before the act was annulled for violating the federal Constitution,[122] the Chinese struggled to gain a secure foothold in their adopted country.[123] In one northern California town, named (of all things) Locke, the Chinese found a way around the state's limitations on ownership. In 1915, after a series of race riots drove them out of cities all along the West Coast, Chinese immigrants found refuge on nine acres of land owned by the family of George Locke, a Sacramento carpet merchant and pear farmer. The family leased the land, about a half hour south of Sacramento, at $5 per house and $10 per store.[124] Thus was born the town of Locke (pronounced "Lock-ee") a flourishing little city and the only all-Chinese town on the Sacramento Delta. There were no police and no formal government, only a traditional Chinese corporation, called a tong, to settle disputes between citizens. There were three gambling halls and five brothels, and yet for 50 years Locke was, for the most part, a peaceful and pleasant community.

At the end of World War II, the younger generation began to move out, and the city began a gradual decline. The courts finally declared the Alien Land Act unconstitutional in 1952, but since none of the residents could afford the expense associated with subdividing the land into individual plots, they could still not buy the ground under their stores and homes.

Today Locke is quietly deteriorating, and, ironically, restrictions on property rights are largely to blame. In 1977 the Sacramento Housing and Development Authority began planning to restrict any change to the buildings, intending to maintain Locke as a historic site. But while the plans were in the works, the land was purchased by a Hong Kong company that intended to develop it as a tourist attraction.[125] Worried that the company might turn the area into a sort of amusement park, Sacramento County passed an ordinance declaring Locke a "special planning area" and prohibiting bars, taverns, liquor stores, massage parlors, card rooms, and billboards— all of which had historically been the town's most successful enterprises. Those ordinances, write local historians Jeff Gillenkirk and James Motlow, have stifled attempts to rescue the town from decay and disintegration. "Restrictions on the type and intensity of development within the existing town mean that a private developer wishing to make money on Locke would have to expand any project into surrounding lands. Yet all such plans have run counter to existing zoning regulations."[126] As a result, the town sits in limbo, much of it vacant, some of the buildings collapsing.

40

But there is reason for hope. In 2002 the owner sold the property to the city government, which subdivided it and resold it to the residents in December 2004. For the first time, the Chinese could own the land of their refuge. Connie King, an 81-year-old widow who came to Locke in 1949, was asked how she felt when she took title to the home where she and her husband had raised three children. "I am born here," she said. "I am American citizen. I should be qualified to own the land. . . . I know I'll feel different. I'll own something."[127]

The story of what happened to Dr. Ossian Sweet's Detroit dream house in the fall of 1925 has a similarly dramatic ending.[128] A black obstetrician who graduated from Howard University and studied in Paris with Marie Curie, Sweet got a job at a local black hospital and bought a brick-faced bungalow in a middle-class Detroit neighborhood where he hoped to live with his wife Gladys and daughter Iva. But Sweet and his colleagues faced serious obstacles to their American dream. Only a few months earlier, one of Sweet's colleagues, Dr. Alexander Turner, had moved into a home in a wealthy Detroit suburb. On moving day, Turner's home was surrounded by a crowd of more than 100 screaming whites, outraged that a black family would move into "their" neighborhood.[129] Two white men banged on the door, pretending to be police officers, and when Turner let them in, they pointed a gun at his head and forced him to sign the home over to them. Then the mob ordered the family outside, loaded their furniture into a van, and threw rocks at their windshield as they drove away. Two weeks later, a race riot erupted when a black undertaker moved into a home in another neighborhood.[130] After the Ku Klux Klan held a rally attended by as many as 10,000 people, the mayor urged blacks not to move into white neighborhoods "simply to gratify [their] personal pride."[131]

Well aware of such incidents, Sweet took precautions for his own moving day on September 9. He asked 10 friends and family members to help him and Gladys move in, and he brought along firearms just in case. Some time around sunset, a crowd surrounded the house, shouting and throwing rocks. Although police officers had been stationed at the house to protect the Sweets, the officers did nothing to disperse the crowd. When Dr. Sweet's brother Otis arrived in a taxicab, the mob surged forward, throwing rocks and shouting "Niggers, get the niggers!" As the tension and violence rose, a shot rang out, followed by several more. Moments later the police rushed in and arrested everyone in the house on charges of murder: a white man across the street had been killed by a stray bullet.

The NAACP rushed to the Sweets' defense. Intercepting Clarence Darrow as he traveled home from the famous *Scopes* trial, they pleaded with him to defend Sweet. Darrow accepted. Over the course of that fall—and again after the first trial ended in a mistrial—Darrow and his co-counsel, ACLU lawyer Arthur Garfield Hays, argued that blacks had as much right to defend their families and homes as whites did. Hays began his opening statement by reciting a famous description of property rights by English prime minister William Pitt: "The poorest man may in his cottage bid defiance to all the forces of the Crown; it may be frail, its roof may shake, the wind may blow through it; the storm may enter, the rain may enter; but the King of England cannot enter; all his forces dare not cross the threshold of that ruined tenement." Self-defense, Hays continued, "is the dearest right of a free man. Anything less than the right to use the fullest measure of protection when home and life are threatened would be contrary to human nature."[132]

The trial was rough going at first. All of the police officers testified that there was no crowd, just a few stragglers, and that nobody had thrown any rocks. Neighbors testified that they "couldn't remember" whether they were members of the local KKK, and more than 50 prosecution witnesses claimed that while the police were carefully keeping order, the residents of the house had fired indiscriminately out of the windows. But Darrow managed to get a prosecution witness to admit that police officers had coached him, and when the defense's turn came, Darrow expertly proved that Sweet and his family had been met by a crowd of infuriated whites, that his colleagues had been forced from their homes, and that the Sweets' case was only one example of a long history of oppression. "When I opened the door," Dr. Sweet testified, "I realized that I was facing that same mob that had hounded my people through its entire history. I realized my back was against the wall and I was filled with a peculiar type of fear—the fear of one who knows the history of my race."[133]

When the first trial ended in a hung jury, Sweet and the others were retried. After a new jury heard the evidence, Judge Frank Murphy—who would rise to become a justice on the U.S. Supreme

Court—turned to them with instructions. "Under the law," he said, "a man's house is his castle. It is his castle, whether he is white or black, and no man has the right to assault or invade it ... every man has the right to defend the possession of his home and his person, and the persons of his family or his dependents."[134] After deliberating only three hours, the jury found the defendants not guilty.[135] But Sweet's life was never the same. Gladys contracted tuberculosis while in jail and infected their infant daughter, who died later that year. Gladys herself died two years later. When Ossian went to the cemetery for her funeral, he was confronted by guards who told him that blacks had to enter through the back gate. He pulled a revolver on them and led his wife's funeral procession through the front gate.[136] He remarried and remained in the house until selling it in 1944.

Of course, racism has many causes, and effective enforcement of property rights will not eradicate it. But property rights help insulate minorities against exploitation by prejudiced majorities. That is why racists have often focused their attacks on the rights of unpopular groups to own and use property.

A world without property rights would be one in which some of the worst traits of human beings would be indulged. Rather than reward hard work, integrity, and ingenuity, a society without property would reward the strong, the ruthless, and the conniving. Earlier in this chapter I quoted Cass Sunstein's claim that privacy and property rights are "creations of law" and that "without the law of trespass, and accompanying legal rules of contract and tort, the relationship between employers and employees would not be what it now is; indeed, it would be extremely difficult to figure out what that relationship might be."[137] But in fact it is *not* hard to see what such relationships would be like. When Venezuelan dictator Hugo Chavez seized Venezuela's Coca-Cola bottling plants, a reporter described the scene that followed when employees protested:

> Images broadcast live on three television networks showed the troops throwing the protesters, most of them women, to the ground and then kicking cans of tear gas at them. In an interview with reporters, the officer in charge of the action, Gen. Luis Felipe Acosta Carles, taunted the news media and insulted plant managers. News reports said workers at the plants were beaten.

"We are distributing this product to the population because collective rights come above individual rights," Acosta said, slurping down a warm soft drink and belching into the camera. "What I see here is hoarding, and we are going to move these products."

Troops later pushed their way into a warehouse of the beer and food maker Empresas Polar, Venezuela's largest private company, also in Carabobo, after forcing managers out into the street.[138]

That sort of civil strife pits neighbors against neighbors in violent confrontation, deters the investment and stability that make for a healthy economy, and rewards brutality and ignorance. A country where incidents like this occur is unlikely to generate or receive the foreign investment so important to securing a stable and prosperous economy.

When a country has a reputation for violating property rights, people with money are likely to invert it somewhere else. After Chavez came to power, for example, foreign investment in Venezuela plummeted.[139] Similarly, decades of political instability and government seizure of foreign-owned investments have left the Democratic Republic of Congo in bad shape. "Organized capital markets and most credit instruments typically found on financial markets are virtually non-existent in Congo," declared a recent U.S. Embassy report.[140] And in yet another example, the government of Zimbabwe recently began a policy of "land reform," seizing farms owned by whites and transferring them to blacks. As a result, writes Craig J. Richardson, "Zimbabwe went from a place of hope to one of the grimmest places on earth." The gross domestic product fell by 18 percent within three years, inflation skyrocketed to 500 percent, and between 1998 and 2001 foreign investment fell by 99 percent.[141]

Even in the United States, a lack of security for private property rights can harm the economy. When inner cities suffer from extensive property crime, such as vandalism and theft, people invest their money elsewhere. Businesses avoid those places where new investment, and with it new jobs, are the most needed. Although cities frequently try to use subsidies and tax breaks to entice businesses to locate in inner cities, the most important thing a city can do to foster economic growth is to ensure that people who put their savings into a new business won't lose their investments to crime—or to city hall.

In addition to deterring investment, a society without property rights would be unable to figure out how to use whatever resources it might have. As we saw earlier, with Mises' example of the railroad, private property and exchange are essential for people who need to make decisions and plan for the future. Without property, people would be unable to choose where to invest their time and energy, or how much of a product or good to provide, or where their efforts would be most efficiently spent. A society that did not respect property rights might still be able to make some decisions, but those decisions would have no *economic* dimension. Instead, they would be based on considerations of power—that is, on *political* considerations. Questions about how to use time and resources would be decided primarily by influence and authority and only incidentally by the knowledge, choices, or desires of producers and consumers.

Making choices on the basis of political influence instead of what producers and consumers need is a typical consequence of the weakening of private property rights. Whenever government has the power to put burdens on some people, or give benefits to other people, citizens will begin to spend their time and energy trying to convince the government to give those benefits to *them*. The more government undermines property rights and redistributes assets between groups, the more lobbying will go on. Such lobbying is already a multi-billion-dollar industry in the United States. Every year companies and special interests invest billions in the effort to convince government to give them even more billions. Economists call this "rent seeking."

Rent seeking can be explained by a simple thought experiment. Suppose I have the power to take a $1 "tax" from each person in a group of 50 people and then give that $50 as a gift to one of my three best friends. How much will each of my friends spend trying to convince me to give the money to him? Keeping in mind that, statistically, each of them has only a one-third chance of success, they will each spend one-third of $50, or $16.67. Meanwhile, each of the 50 people I took the dollars from will only spend *99 cents* on their efforts to convince me not to *take away* their dollars—they would end up losing even more if they spent more than that.

As this thought experiment shows, rent seeking tends to have a ratchet effect, which increases wealth redistribution over time. First, because each of the victims of my "tax" has only a dollar at stake, they find that they would rather lose that one dollar than spend their time and energy organizing to oppose my redistribution program; meanwhile, my three friends have as much as $50 at stake, so they will take the issue much more seriously. Second, some of the people who were $1 "taxpayers" the first time around will probably try to become my friends, hoping for a chance at a payoff the next time I choose to redistribute money.

Rent seeking has many unfortunate consequences. For one thing, it wastes time and money because it distracts businesses from producing the goods and services that people need. Instead of producing more and better goods and services, people waste time quarreling over what has already been produced. Companies spend their income hiring lobbyists and taking politicians out to lunch instead of developing new vaccines, safer cars, faster airplanes, or more nutritious food.[142] Worse, the lobbying game tends to be won by those groups that are already wealthy and popular; poor people, and members of unpopular minorities, rarely persuade the government to do their bidding. They are generally too busy working to spend their day talking to politicians and don't have the resources to compete against well-organized interest groups.

Without property rights, disputes would not be settled by contracts or mutual agreement; they would be solved by force. And when property rights are weakened, disputes are settled by a softer variety of force: politics. The poor, and people without political connections, would have little chance of succeeding in the lobbying game, no matter how worthy they might be.

Thanks largely to the erosion of property rights, rent seeking is already an epidemic in America. Eminent domain is regularly used against poor minority or ethnic communities and in favor of wealthy and politically influential corporations. In 1999 the city of Lancaster, California, condemned a 99 Cents Only store to transfer the property to Costco. There was *already* a Costco in that shopping mall, but the mega-retailer wanted to expand, so it persuaded the city to act.[143] The property was not deteriorating, the company admitted, but it might in the future, and the city could prevent "future blight" by condemning the store and transferring it to Costco now. Politicians quickly complied. When the 99 Cents Only store went to court, the judge was surprised to hear city officials openly admit they were working on behalf of a private company: "By Lancaster's own admissions, it was willing to go to any lengths—even so far as condemning commercially

46

viable, unblighted real property—simply to keep Costco within the city's boundaries."[144] The city's only desire, the court noted, was "to appease Costco." But there was nothing wrong with that, the city argued. After all, government exists to foster the development of business, and Costco is a major business.

Although the court ruled against the city and allowed the 99 Cents Only store to remain, few other condemnations end so happily. In case after case, interest groups with greater political influence convince courts to transfer property in ways that benefit them, at the expense of groups that have less political pull—often racial minorities and the poor. When residents of Boynton Beach, Florida, learned that their elected officials were considering a redevelopment plan that would condemn several properties and replace them with more upscale shopping and recreational facilities, they demanded answers. The city council held a special meeting to explain the proposal. In a presentation titled "Why Are We Doing This?" the director of the city's redevelopment agency told the city council that although Boynton Beach and nearby Delray Beach had similar populations,

> when comparing median household incomes, Boynton Beach ranks lower at $39,845 than Delray at $43,371.... The purpose of this redevelopment, is to compensate for the loss of one of the City's major taxpayers. Our property tax values are meager compared to other cities and this redevelopment is our attempt to enhance property values.... In Boynton Beach, there is a significant amount of property that pays little or no taxes. Given that reality, we must do other things to compensate for that loss of tax dollars.[145]

In other words, if you kick poor people out of the city, there won't be any poor people in the city. Well, that is certainly true. But it is hardly just.

In the 1960s and 1970s, under the mantle of "urban renewal," countless poor neighborhoods were razed to make way for middle-class homes and shopping centers, a process that fell hardest on black property owners. Urban renewal, which its victims came to call "Negro removal," was a technique whereby government could "clean up the neighborhood" by ordering "undesirable" classes out of an area to make way for landowners that those in power preferred.[146] Likewise, the rent-seeking problem today shows that the minority is always at a disadvantage. When lobbyists compete for the opportunity to use government force for their own purposes, the winners are those lobbyists who are most influential; power tends to fall into the hands, not of the most hardworking or the most needy, but of the most politically adept.

A society without property rights, or with weakened property rights, turns into a political free-for-all in which competing private interest groups battle for the opportunity to use government power for their own benefit. Often those groups say—and sincerely believe—that their projects are in the interest of the general public; indeed, redevelopment projects are commonly supported by most of the people in a city, who hope that the projects will "create jobs" or improve the local economy. But property rights are supposed to protect the minority against the majority—after all, if we must get the approval of voters before we are allowed to keep our homes and businesses, we have only *permissions*, not *rights*.

A world without property rights would be a world with few incentives to produce and create, no way to save for the future or insure against emergencies, and no way to secure our privacy. It would be a world where no house would be a home, where no church could protect itself from its enemies, and where dissent would carry a very high price indeed. It would be a world where jealousy, contempt, and laziness would not be deterred; where foresight, intelligence, hard work, and careful planning would not be rewarded. It would be a world without treasured possessions like wedding rings, old photographs, heirloom furniture, antique clocks, or commemorative pins. It would be a world where sentimental value would count for nothing, where the moral significance of the things we earn would not be respected, and where generosity and kindness—no longer a matter of choice—would not be rewarded with gratitude. The poorest members of such a society might benefit temporarily by being able to take things they wanted from others. But since there would be no reward for making new things, the stores would soon run dry. Without "good fences," neighbors would come into increasing conflict; without places where people could go to "be themselves," they would feel increasingly stifled, isolated, and ignored. Without the ability to exclude others from their sanctuaries, people would have less chance to express their feelings of intimacy. Without the ability to forge themselves into groups with others who share their values, they would feel increasingly lonesome. Without the

48

ability to save, they would be unable to plan their lives. Society would be unable to make long-range plans, and investment decisions would be based, not on the more productive uses of time and money, but on the basis of the more politically popular uses of time and money. In short, it would be a society where the noblest aspects of human life would go unrewarded and the worst would receive every indulgence. Nothing would have value—and nothing would be priceless.

Few people today advocate the complete abolition of private property rights. Instead, they argue that government should *limit* property rights, either by regulating what people may do with their land or by seizing it through eminent domain and giving it to others to use more productively. Often, such people speak of "balancing" property rights with the "needs of society," or say, as the *New York Times* did after the Supreme Court's *Kelo* decision was announced, that the ends justify the means. Taking away people's homes, the *Times* editorialized, "may hurt a few small property owners . . . but many residents are likely to benefit."[147] But diminishing property rights causes many of the same effects as abolishing them, only on a smaller scale. As the *Pappas* and *Mesdaq* cases show, weakening property rights decreases freedom, making it harder for people to plan for the future or to be secure in their homes or businesses. Moreover, as the *Poletown* case reveals, interfering with property rights increases wasteful rent seeking and makes it harder for neighbors to trust one another. And as the *Bugryn* case demonstrates, forcing people to give up their property for the "greater good" of society can lead to cynicism and the erosion of democratic values.

Good fences make good neighbors, but limiting property rights means lowering those fences. In the eyes of the *Times*'s editorial writers, property is not really a right but a permission, which can be revoked whenever political leaders decide that doing so will "benefit" others. But that attitude leaves us at the mercy of lobbyists and politicians—and transforms government from a peacekeeper into a real estate agent. That was not what America's Founding Fathers had in mind.

3. The Place of Property Rights in the American Constitution

America's Founders understood the vital role that property rights play in human life, both individually and socially, and they wrote a constitution that included several important protections for private property. In recent years, however, those protections have been ignored, denigrated, and swept aside. To be true to our Constitution and the principles of justice on which it is based, those protections should be understood, appreciated, and enforced.

Understanding the role that property plays in the American Constitution requires us first to consider some deeper questions about government itself. Why does government exist? The question is a controversial one, of course. In fact, many political philosophers believe that there is no such thing as a "purpose" for government in the first place—government just *is*; there's no "why" about it. But the 17th-century political philosopher Thomas Hobbes believed that there was a purpose for government, and he proposed to discover what it was by imagining what the world would be like without government. He called such a world "the state of nature." In a state of nature, strong people would go about beating up weaker people and taking away their things. Life in such a society would be "solitary, poor, nasty, brutish, and short"[1]—and people would have no way of defending themselves except through violence. But while such an existence would certainly be unpleasant, Hobbes did not believe there was anything *wrong* with it. Justice, he argued, is always based on the assertions of someone with power. If there is no power to create and enforce rules, then there is no such thing as justice itself—and therefore, in the state of nature, there is really no reason that robbery would be *wrong* until a government declared it to be so. "Where there is no common power, there is no law: where no law, no injustice."[2]

Because life in the state of nature is so unpleasant, Hobbes continued, people would come together to create a government to protect themselves. But without any prepolitical definition of justice, whatever the government chose to define as just or unjust would automatically become so. "Justice" and "law" are therefore *the same thing*. That means that there are no limits to what sort of government may be created—and no limit to what the government may do to the people. If the sovereign takes our things away, we have no right to complain; the fact that the sovereign does it automatically makes it just.

John Locke rejected that argument. He, too, believed that people create government to protect themselves from the bullies who would harm them in the state of nature, but unlike Hobbes, he held that there is such a thing as justice even before government comes into being. "The state of nature has a law of nature to govern it," he said, "and reason . . . is that law." Under the law of nature, theft is simply wrong, and even people who do not know of such things as government understand that theft is wrong because "truth, and keeping of faith belongs to men as men, and not as members of society." Thus government does not *create* justice; it merely recognizes and enforces natural rules of right and wrong.

Under those natural rules, each person has the right to run his own life, and it is that right that government is created to protect. The purpose of the law, Locke wrote, is *"to preserve and enlarge freedom."* But preserving freedom means not only allowing people to act and speak as they will; it also means recognizing each person's *"liberty* to dispose and order freely as he lists his person, actions, possessions, and his whole property within the allowance of those laws under which he is, and therein not to be subject to the arbitrary will of another, but freely follow his own." For Locke, this liberty flowed from a person's right to run his own life: that is why Locke used the word "property" as a "general name" for people's "lives, liberties, and estates." A person owns his home, his body and his beliefs and has the right to do with them what he wishes.

At the same time that it authorizes government to protect life, liberty, and estate, the law of nature limits what government may do. Since people have no *right* to steal things from one another in a state of nature, they also may not ask the government to steal on their behalf; if they were to do so, they would find themselves once again subject to the arbitrary will of each other, just as they were in the state of nature before government was created. The power of the legislature is only "the joint power of every member of the society," and "nobody has an absolute arbitrary power . . . [to] take away the life or property of another."[7] Therefore, nobody may delegate to the government that kind of power. The government exists "for the preservation of property," which means ensuring that people do not intrude on each other's rights.[8]

The Founders' Vision

The American Founders were powerfully inspired by Locke's ideas. Like him, they believed that government is bound by moral laws that have some deeper meaning than mere force and violence. Thomas Jefferson, for example, wrote that "the people in mass . . . are inherently independent of all *but moral* law."[9] The Declaration of Independence holds that the united colonies may only "do . . . [t]hings which Independent States may *of right* do"[10]—not absolutely anything, but only those things they may do *of right*—and that government derives its *just* powers only from the consent of the governed. James Madison, the father of the Constitution, was more thorough. The power of the majority, he wrote, was only the power to do "anything that could be *rightfully* done by the unanimous concurrence of the members." People reserve some rights to themselves when they enter into society, and those rights, including religious freedom, are "beyond the legitimate reach of sovereignty."[11] In other words, government is really just a group of people entrusted with limited power for certain reasons and within certain boundaries. Government officials must obey the same rules when dealing with us that other people must obey; constitutional law limits their treatment of us just as tort law regulates the way that private citizens may interact with us—their authority is limited by our rights.

Locke described individual rights as all deriving from a common principle: the exclusive right to own and to use our *selves*. Locke saw property as the comprehensive term for all rights. Everyone "has a *property* in his own *person*. This nobody has any right to but himself."[12] Since the "*labour* of his body and the *work* of his hands" belong to him, he may do with them what he pleases, and keep the fruits of his industry—a principle Frederick Douglass would understand so clearly in 19th-century Baltimore. When people make things, or trade their work for wages, or spend their wages on things, they have a right to those things because they have invested their personalities in them. For the same reason, people have property in their minds, their opinions, and their personalities. For another person to demand that someone give up "the *labour* of his body and the *work* of his hands" or the goods and services that he trades them for, or to prohibit him from investing his money in a commercial enterprise, or to censor his free speech, or to forbid him from worshipping would subject the victim to inequality and servitude. As Jefferson argued: "If we are made in some degree for others, yet in a greater [degree] are we made for ourselves. It were contrary to feeling and indeed ridiculous to suppose that a man had less right in himself than one of his neighbors or indeed all of them put together. This would be slavery."[13]

Law prevents other people—whether as individuals or in groups—from arbitrarily interfering with our lives, by preventing or punishing those who would violate our rightful possessions, our lives, or our liberties. Locke emphasized that freedom is not the absence of law; on the contrary, freedom is the goal to be preserved through law.

> [T]he end of law is not to abolish or restrain, but to preserve and enlarge freedom. . . . [F]or liberty [means], to be free from restraint and violence from others; which cannot be, where there is no law: but freedom is not, as we are told, a liberty for every man to do what he lists: (for who could be free, when every other man's humour might domineer over him?) but a liberty to dispose, and order as he lists, his person, actions, possessions, and his whole property, within the allowance of those laws under which he is, and therein not to be subject to the arbitrary will of another, but freely follow his own.[14]

In a brilliant little essay called, simply, "Property," James Madison summed up the Lockean position succinctly: "Government is instituted to protect property of every sort; as well that which lies in the various rights of individuals, as that which the term particularly expresses. This being the end of government, that alone is a *just* government, which *impartially* secures to every man, whatever is his *own*."[15]

It bears emphasizing that the founding generation rarely defended the concept of private property on the basis of its economic consequences. The greater prosperity of societies that respected property rights was seen as a *confirmation*, not as the *origin*, of the basic justice of private property rights. Private property, they believed, was not so much the right to the particular things a person possessed as it was a manifestation of that person's fundamental right to pursue happiness and earn a living for himself and his family.[16] The French philosopher Destutt de Tracy, whose work Thomas Jefferson admired and translated into English, explained that a person is inescapably attached to the ownership of his own body and mind, things which make up a person's individuality.[17] And a person's dominion over his body means that he can employ that self in exchange for gain: the right to liberty means that a person may use his talents and skill to provide for his own subsistence. The right to keep and use the things a person earns therefore guarantees that person's liberty. As an anonymous patriot wrote in the *Boston Gazette*, "*Liberty* and *Property* are not only join'd in common discourse, but are in their own natures so nearly ally'd, that we cannot be said to possess the one without the enjoyment of the other."[18] The Virginia Declaration of Rights echoed that sentiment, noting that among the "certain inherent rights" that all people have are "the enjoyment of life and liberty, with the means of acquiring and possessing property, and pursuing and obtaining happiness and safety."[19] Property rights, argued John Trenchard in the influential *Cato's Letters*, derive from the liberty of a person to use his faculties as he chooses:

> [A]ll Men are animated by the Passion of acquiring and defending Property, because Property is the best Support of that Independency, so passionately desired by all Men. Even Men the most dependent have it constantly in their Heads and their Wishes, to become independent one Time or other; and the Property which they are acquiring, or mean to acquire by that Dependency, is intended to bring them out of it, and to procure them an agreeable Independency. And as Happiness is the Effect of Independency, and Independency the Effect of Property; so certain Property is the Effect of Liberty alone, and can only be secured by the Laws of Liberty. . . .[20]

It is this understanding of property rights that explains why Thomas Jefferson rephrased the classic Lockean trinity, "life, liberty, and property," as "life, liberty and the pursuit of happiness" in the Declaration of Independence. Jefferson was making clear that the fundamental rights of mankind include the right to use one's liberty in pursuit of one's own goals and that property rights are a manifestation of the fundamental right of liberty. According to Jefferson, "[T]he first principle of association" is "the guarantee to every one of a free exercise of his industry, and the fruits acquired by it."[21] Life, liberty, and property are essentially the same idea seen from three different time perspectives: the present tense of self-ownership is the right to life; the future tense is the right to liberty, the right to act in the future; and the past tense of self-ownership is the right to property, the right to keep the fruits of our self-investment. As Madison summed it up, "The personal right to acquire property, which is a natural right, gives to property, when acquired, a right to protection, as a social right."[22]

In addition to the importance of property rights in preserving every person's right to pursue happiness, Madison and his contemporaries understood that property rights are a necessary foundation for a healthy society. If a nation began to abrogate property rights, or to redistribute property equally among all the people, the result would be not harmony but chaos. "The idle, the vicious, the intemperate, would rush into the utmost extravagance of debauchery, sell and spend all their share, and then demand a new division of those who purchased from them," wrote John Adams. "The moment that the idea is admitted into society that property is not as sacred as the laws of God . . . anarchy and tyranny commence."[23] James Wilson, one of the authors of the U.S. Constitution, agreed. Without private property, he wrote, "the tranquility of society would be perpetually disturbed by fierce and ungovernable competitions for the possession and enjoyment of things, insufficient to satisfy all, and by no rules of adjustment distributed to each."[24] As Eric Claeys concludes, America's Founders understood that property rights are essential to a civil, safe society because they "teach and habituate citizens to see their fellow citizens not as rivals but as neighbors and potential friends." The basic rapport on which tranquil civilization rests "cannot flourish unless people first feel secure that they can take care of their most basic needs of survival and, more generally, that none of their would-be friends will interfere with their own. . . . Trite as it may sound, good fences make good neighbors."[25]

Relying on those principles, the Founders drafted a constitution that simultaneously authorized and limited the government's authority. Congress, it declared, would have only those specific powers "herein granted," and those powers would be narrowed further by limits written into the original Constitution, as well as the Bill of Rights, which was added later.

There are at least three separate amendments in the Bill of Rights that refer directly to the right of private property. The Third Amendment forbids the government from stationing military troops in private homes. One of the American Revolutionaries' leading complaints against the king was that he forced homeowners to take in British soldiers, and the Declaration of Independence even cited this as one of George III's abuses. The Fourth Amendment declares that the people have the right "to be secure in their persons, houses, papers, and effects, against unreasonable searches and seizures." When the police suspect a crime has been committed, they must get the approval of an impartial judge before intruding into our private places and possessions.

Most important of all, the Fifth Amendment declares, "No person shall be . . . deprived of life, liberty, or property, without due process of law; nor shall private property be taken for public use, without just compensation."

As lawyers of the founding generation well knew, the phrase "due process of law" derives from Magna Carta, which declared in one particularly famous passage, "No freeman shall be taken, or imprisoned, or disseised, or outlawed, or exiled, or in any way harmed— nor will we go upon or send upon him—save by the lawful judgment of his peers or by the law of the land."[26] The "law of the land" provision meant that the king could take a subject's property only as punishment for some specified public infraction, for violating some generally applicable rule instituted for the public good. The phrase was an attempt to ensure a measure of generality in the government's use of coercion: the king could use the state's powers for the benefit of all of the people but not for his own aggrandizement or that of his cronies.

For Locke's followers, this generality principle was especially important, because it helped to distinguish legitimate uses of force from illegitimate ones. Since government exists to protect us all from people who would forcibly deprive us of our lives, liberties, and property, the government must not itself become an instrument for such injustice. As Madison put it in *Federalist* 51, "In framing a government which is to be administered by men over men, the great difficulty lies in this: you must first enable the government to control the governed; and in the next place oblige it to control itself."[27] For government to forbid robbery, for example, is legitimate because it protects the rights of all without interfering with legitimate freedoms. But a government decree that takes away the property of some simply to benefit others is essentially the same as robbery, which perverts the state and turns it from its natural purposes. A good analogy would be to a security guard at a bank. So long as he protects the bank from robbers, his use of force is legitimate, because it is within the rightful scope of his employment. But if he uses his gun to rob the bank, he has betrayed his employer's trust and lost his legitimate authority, regardless of the fact that he still wears a badge. When government does the same thing, by using force not for legitimate, public reasons but for merely private reasons, it, too, is betraying a trust. Such actions are essentially arbitrary, and thus do not qualify as law. The "due process *of law*" clause forbids the government to take the lives, liberty, or property of some groups merely for the enrichment or private satisfaction of other groups or individuals.

The distinction between law and arbitrary force was important to the Framers; as James Madison put it:

> [T]here is no maxim . . . more liable to be misapplied . . . than the . . . one that the interest of the majority is the political standard of right and wrong. Taking the word "interest" as synonymous with "Ultimate happiness," in which sense it is qualified with every necessary moral ingredient, the proposition is no doubt true. But taking it in the popular sense, as referring to immediate augmentation of property and wealth, nothing can be more false. In the latter sense it would be the interest of the majority in every community to despoil & enslave the minority of individuals. . . . In fact it is only reestablishing under another name and a more specious form, force as the measure of right.[28]

In *Calder v. Bull*,[29] Justice Samuel Chase explained that the generality requirement prohibited government from passing legislation that merely transferred property from one person to another. "The purposes for which men enter into society . . . determine the nature and terms of the social compact," wrote Chase, and those purposes include the protection of their property from intrusion by other people. Thus the "vital principles in our free Republican governments" do not allow the legislature to "take away that security for personal liberty, or private property, for the protection whereof the government was established." Such an attempt would be an act of arbitrary force, not a law; therefore it would deprive a person of property without due process *of law*: "An ACT of the Legislature (for I cannot call it a law) contrary to the great first principles of the social compact, cannot be considered a rightful exercise of legislative authority." Legislation that "takes property from A. and gives it to B" contradicts the whole purpose of government and violates the Due Process Clause because it is enacted for private and not for public reasons.[30] In the 20th century, this theory would come to be called "substantive due process."

Involuntary government redistributions of property among *private* parties being absolutely forbidden, the Fifth Amendment then goes on to proclaim what government must do when it takes property for *public* use. In such cases, the government must provide just compensation to the owner. This ensures that the government's power to take property does not lay the entire cost of public projects disproportionately on individual citizens, or create special profits for those people who are more popular with government authorities.[31]

Unfortunately, there were at least two glaring instances in which the young American nation betrayed the principles of private property on which it was based: the treatment of Native Americans and slavery. Contrary to the popular romantic myth, American Indian tribes had sophisticated social systems including strong notions of private property.[32] The Cherokees, for example, were not primitive savages; they embraced many social and technical innovations, including newspapers published in their own language, a public education system, and a written constitution.[33] But as 19th-century American farmers encroached more and more on Cherokee-owned land in Georgia and Tennessee, conflict between natives and settlers reached crisis levels. When the state of Georgia pressed its policy of confiscating Cherokee land, the tribe responded, not by going to war, but by filing a lawsuit in the U.S. Supreme Court.[34] Chief Justice John Marshall ruled that the Cherokees were "the undisputed possessors of the soil"[35] and that state interference with that right was unconstitutional.[36] President Jackson, however, refused to enforce the ruling.[37] With the law thus ignored, state and federal authorities rounded up the Cherokees and deported them to the west, on what came to be known as "The Trail of Tears." Far from demonstrating the injustice of the American Constitution, the Cherokee experience testifies to the importance of property rights and the awful consequences of ignoring the Constitution's protections.

Slavery was an even more egregious betrayal of the basic principles of property. Since the basis of the American Founders' philosophy was that each person had an equal right to self-ownership, it was a glaring hypocrisy for some people to own others, and the founding generation knew it. Jefferson,[38] Madison,[39] and Washington[40] were haunted by the perversity of a slave-owning society, and George Mason refused to sign the Constitution in part because of its compromises with slavery.[41] Yet others felt the political power of slavery's supporters could not be overcome. In his original draft of the Declaration of Independence, Jefferson had included a furious denunciation of slavery. The king of England had "waged cruel war against human nature itself, violating it's [sic] most sacred rights of life and liberty" by enslaving "a distant people who never offended him." This "piratical warfare," which Jefferson claimed was even "the opprobrium of *infidel* powers," was nevertheless carried on by "the *Christian* king of Great Britain"—here Jefferson underlined "Christian" and printed it in large letters, instead of using cursive. The king was "determined to keep open a market where MEN should be bought and sold"—the only instance of emphatic capitals in Jefferson's draft. Yet his strong feelings failed to carry the day, and the passage was removed at the insistence of delegates from South Carolina and Georgia.[42]

Likewise, the Constitution was riddled with compromises on slavery, including a peculiar compromise that counted only three-fifths of the population of slaves when apportioning representatives among the population. That "federal ratio" struck a bizarre middle ground on the nature of slaves as people or as property, while another clause imposed a 20-year moratorium on any law banning the international slave trade.[43] Still, James Madison remained insistent on one point: the word "slave" would not appear in the Constitution because "Mr. Madison thought it wrong to admit in the Constitution the idea that there could be property in men."[44] Nevertheless, the wealth represented by the unjust "property" of slaveholders was a powerful obstacle to reform—an obstacle too powerful, in many cases, for many of America's most conscientious Founders. In 1791, when the well-known Quaker abolitionist Robert Pleasants asked Madison to introduce a petition against slavery in the House of Representatives, Madison refused, explaining that it would "giv[e] a public wound . . . to an interest on which [slaveholders] set so great a value."[45] In all, the founding experience with slavery was one of tragic compromise, putting off to a future generation the solution to one of the world's great crimes.

The Civil War Amendments

In the years that followed, abolitionists such as William Lloyd Garrison and Frederick Douglass articulated their demand for equal freedom of all—a demand grounded on the right to the property in one's own person. We have seen how Douglass viewed slavery as a fundamental violation of private property rights. The "all-consuming duty of the American people," he argued, was "to give the slave to *himself*."[46] Other abolitionists, too, insisted that blacks had the same right to own themselves and the product of their labor as whites did, and one of slavery's primary evils was that it violated this essential truth.[47] In his epochal speech "The Barbarism of Slavery," Charles Sumner denounced "a system which . . . sordidly takes from the slave all the fruits of his bitter sweat, and thus takes from him the mainspring to exertion." Slavery's essence lay "in the appropriation of all the toil of its victims, excluding them from that property in their own earnings, which the law of nature allows, and civilization secures. . . . It is robbery and petty larceny under the garb of law."[48]

Abolitionists attacked slavery for violating a person's right to the ownership of his or her own body.[49] "Freeing the slave," declared the American Anti-Slavery Society in 1833, "is not depriving [southerners] of property, but restoring it to its rightful owner."[50] Theodore Weld concurred: "A man's right to himself is his only absolute right—his right to anything else is relative to this, is derived from it, and held only by virtue of it. *Self-right* [i.e., self-ownership] is the *foundation right*—the *post in the middle*, to which all other rights are fastened."[51] Even Chief Justice John Marshall had acknowledged that "slavery is contrary to the law of nature" because "every man has a natural right to the fruits of his own labor . . . and no other

61

person can rightfully deprive him of those fruits, and expropriate them against his will."[52]

At the close of the Civil War, radical Republicans sought a way to erase the vestiges of slavery remaining in the American union. Among other things, they passed the Civil Rights Act of 1866. That act—the first of its kind in America—placed a heavy emphasis on property rights. It declared that all people, regardless of race, would have the same right "to inherit, purchase, lease, sell, hold, and convey real and personal property, and to full and equal benefit of all laws and proceedings for the security of person and property, as is enjoyed by white citizens. . . ."[53] But when President Andrew Johnson vetoed the act—declaring that it exceeded Congress's authority—Congress overrode his veto and then drafted the Fourteenth Amendment, in part to ensure the act's constitutionality. The amendment would be the most important change ever made to the American constitutional structure. In 1833 the Supreme Court had found that the Bill of Rights applied only to the federal government.[54] To bring the Bill of Rights to bear against the states, the Fourteenth Amendment was added, prohibiting states from depriving anyone of the "privileges or immunities" of U.S. citizenship, or of "life, liberty, or property without due process of law," or of the "equal protection of the laws."[55]

Those who drafted the amendment explained that the "privileges or immunities" of citizenship included the right to earn and enjoy property. It was based on a clause in the original Constitution that also guaranteed the "privileges and immunities" of citizens and that had been interpreted 43 years earlier, in the case of *Corfield v. Coryell.*[56] The privileges and immunities of American citizens, wrote Supreme Court Justice Bushrod Washington (George Washington's nephew), included those rights "which are, in their nature, fundamental; which belong, of right, to the citizens of all free governments."[57] Among those rights were "the enjoyment of life and liberty, with the right to acquire and possess property of every kind, and to pursue and obtain happiness and safety."[58] By imposing the same language on the states in the new amendment, Reconstruction politicians intended to require states to respect, at a minimum, the fundamental right to pursue happiness by working for a living and keeping the fruits of one's labor. And the addition of a new Due Process of Law Clause meant that states would not have arbitrary power over the people within their jurisdictions.

62

Unfortunately, in the first case ever to interpret the Fourteenth Amendment, the Supreme Court essentially nullified the Privileges or Immunities Clause. In the *Slaughterhouse Cases,*[59] the Court considered a challenge to a Louisiana law granting a monopoly on the New Orleans butchering trade to one privately owned corporation. The independent butchers argued that the law deprived them of the right to earn a living, a right recognized by the common law for centuries.[60] But a bitterly divided five-to-four Court held that the "privileges or immunities of citizens of the United States" included only those rights that appertained to a person's *federal* citizenship, not the rights derived from *state* citizenship, and the right to earn a living derived from *state* citizenship. The new amendment, the Court held, prohibited states from interfering only with federal authority—it did not prohibit states from interfering with the rights of their own citizens.

In dissent, Justice Stephen J. Field noted that the Constitution's supremacy clause already prohibited such interference, so the decision would render the Privileges or Immunities Clause—the most important part of the entire amendment—a "vain and idle enactment."[61] He was prescient: from 1873 to 1999 the Supreme Court enforced the Privileges or Immunities Clause only once, in a decision that was quickly overruled.[62] In 1873 the Court relied on *Slaughterhouse* to uphold a state's power to prohibit women from practicing law,[63] and in that same year, when the sheriff of Grant Parish, Louisiana, led a mob of whites in massacring more than 100 black citizens who were meeting to consider their options after a disputed election, the Supreme Court held that the sheriff could not be prosecuted under federal civil rights laws. The right not to be murdered, the Court held, was not one of the privileges or immunities of federal citizenship.[64] In 1999 the Court indicated that it might be willing to revise its understanding of this clause, but so far it hasn't done so.[65]

With the Privileges or Immunities Clause essentially erased from the Constitution, the Court began to focus on the Due Process Clause instead. In *Loan Association v. Topeka,*[66] the Court considered the constitutionality of a law that invested taxpayer money in a private railroad corporation. The citizens asserted that the law allowed government to take away their money and give it to another private party—a perversion of government authority since it granted benefits to a privileged few instead of protecting everyone equally. The

Court agreed. Government, it held, is created to protect the rights of citizens against those who would harm them or deprive them of their belongings. But government failed in a fundamental way whenever it was taken over by groups that used the state's coercive power to enrich themselves. Most important, it was failing to provide a rule of *law*. Since law is the opposite of arbitrariness, the Due Process Clause requires government to use its power only in the service of some predictable, orderly public goal. The "essential nature of all free governments" puts "limitations on . . . power."[67] But government actions that take the property of some and give it to those able to muster more votes or win political favor transform law into the unpredictable, arbitrary use of force for private, not public, reasons. This makes government into a kind of organized crime.

> To lay with one hand the power of the government on the property of the citizen, and with the other to bestow it upon favored individuals to aid private enterprises and build up private fortunes, is none the less a robbery because it is done under the forms of law and is called taxation. This is not legislation. It is a decree under legislative forms.[68]

And since such enactments would not be law, they would deprive citizens of property without due process *of law*. In the years that followed, this "substantive due process" theory would become one of the most important parts of the Constitution as the Supreme Court increasingly protected citizens against state laws that violated their rights.

The Revenge of Blackstone

Of course, throughout American history there had always been competing interpretations of the role of government. In particular, the Lockean notion that government was inherently limited by the rights of individuals was never without its detractors. In the 1760s the English jurist William Blackstone published his *Commentaries on the Laws of England*, a four-volume explanation of the common law that quickly became one of the great classics in legal literature. But while Blackstone wrote eloquently about individual freedom—and in particular the rights of private property and religious liberty— he differed from John Locke in an important way. Locke had argued that since government was simply a group of people united to protect their rights, it was limited by the same rules that people had to obey when dealing with one another: government had no legitimate authority to murder, steal, or violate other individual rights. But for Blackstone, government was subject to no such limitations. Parliament had "absolute despotic power"[69] and "supreme, irresistible, absolute, uncontrolled authority."[70] It "can, in short, do every thing that is not naturally impossible."[71] Blackstone explicitly rejected the views of "Mr. Locke, and other theoretical writers"[72] regarding the moral limits on government. In his view, government could do anything not specifically prohibited by the Bills of Rights that Parliament had issued, and it could even repeal those.

Blackstone's popularity among law students in early 19th-century America worried some prominent American thinkers, including Thomas Jefferson,[73] James Wilson,[74] and St. George Tucker.[75] When Tucker published an edition of the *Commentaries* in 1803, he added long explanations of the ways in which Blackstone's view of sovereignty clashed with "the new lights which the American revolution has spread over the science of politics."[76] Unlimited sovereignty was simply incompatible with America's founding principles.

Nevertheless, Blackstone's theories gained ground among lawyers, particularly among those lawyers who defended the institution of slavery.[77] That was because Blackstone began with a presumption in favor of governmental authority, which required that a person prove he had the right to be free; that was much more difficult than requiring governing authorities to prove they had the right to deprive a person of freedom.[78] James Madison had proudly asserted that in America, unlike Europe, a person was free to do anything that was not prohibited, instead of having to ask permission from the authorities.[79] But Blackstone reversed this presumption of liberty. Thus, Blackstone allowed later thinkers to avoid the implications of Lockean higher-law principles. If the state were limited by moral law, slavery would be inadmissible; but if the state had supreme and absolute power, and people had only those freedoms that the voters created, there would be nothing to require whites to recognize the natural equality of blacks. In fact, southern intellectual leaders began in the 1830s to attack the Lockean foundation of property rights outright. Where Locke had contended that each person owns himself and that this self-ownership gives each person the right to control his or her own actions, John C. Calhoun and other southern leaders argued that rights are really permissions that society grants to, or withholds from, individuals. The basis of political freedom was not equality or consent at all, Calhoun contended, because man was not really born free and equal. "Individual liberty, or freedom," he declared,

> must be subordinate to whatever power may be necessary to protect society against anarchy within or destruction from without; for the safety and well-being of society is as para-mount to individual liberty, as the safety and well-being of the race is to that of individuals; and in the same proportion, the power necessary for the safety of society is paramount to individual liberty.[80]

Thus, if whites chose to deny blacks freedom, there was nothing wrong with that. Liberty and therefore property were not the effects of a person's moral entitlement to himself; they were social privileges. For Calhoun, property rights were created by society, for its own reasons, and government existed "to preserve and perfect society."[81]

In 1853 the Pennsylvania Supreme Court relied on the Blackstonian theory when it held that the government could invest taxpayer money in a private railroad. Government could do anything that the Constitution did not specifically prohibit, declared Chief Justice Jeremiah Black, a vocal defender of slavery.[82] "In the beginning, the people held in their own hands all the power of an absolute government," he wrote. "The transcendant [sic] powers of Parliament devolved on them by the revolution. . . . If the people of Pennsylvania had given all the authority which they themselves possessed, to a single person, they would have created a despotism as absolute in its control over life, liberty, and property, as that of the Russian autocrat."[83] Locke, of course, had held that such despotic power could never be legitimate, but for Black, the legislature had a "vast" and "supreme" power that could be "limited only by [its] own discretion."

Only a few years later, the California Supreme Court rejected the Blackstonian view of sovereignty when it struck down a law that took property away from absentee landholders and gave it to squatters who were mining on land that didn't belong to them. "It has been erroneously supposed, by many," wrote Justice Hugh C. Murray, "that the Legislature of a State might do any Act, except what was expressly prohibited by the Constitution." That was wrong because government exists "to serve the great ends which that [social] compact was designed to secure, and, hence, it cannot be converted into such an unlimited power, as to defeat the end which mankind had in view, when they entered into the social compact." Since government exists to protect people's property rights, "the spirit of free institutions is at war" with the idea that the government could "take the property of A and give it to B."[84]

But the Blackstonian theory that rights are created by society and that the government may revoke or alter those rights so as to "preserve and protect society" did not die with the end of the Civil War or the ratification of the Fourteenth Amendment. In fact, at the close of the 19th century, the notion that rights are a socially created institution became increasingly popular. Influenced heavily by German philosophers who rejected natural law theories, American political leaders increasingly adopted the principles of pragmatism, which held that not only rights but even the very personalities of individuals are created by society.[85] Morality does not have any necessary connection to the nature of man, these intellectuals argued; rather, it is simply based on social agreement. Now that we had come to understand this fact, older moral and political beliefs—such as the sanctity of individual rights—could be altered in ways that would benefit society.

The philosophy of pragmatism gave rise to the Progressive Movement, a cultural and political crusade that sought to liberate society from what were once considered timeless principles of right and wrong, and to scientifically plan the future of humanity. As historian Louis Menand puts it, the Progressives regarded rights as "socially engineered spaces where parties engaged in specified pursuits enjoy protection from parties who would otherwise naturally seek to interfere. . . . [R]ights are created not for the good of individuals, but for the good of society. Individual freedoms are manufactured to achieve group ends."[86] Louis Brandeis, first a crusading Progressive lawyer and later a justice on the Supreme Court, ridiculed the idea that "industrial combatants" had the right to compete in the marketplace. "I do not wish to be understood as attaching any constitutional or moral sanction to that right. All rights are derived from the purposes of the society in which they exist; above all rights rises duty to the community."[87] Justice Oliver Wendell Holmes put it more simply. Describing an individual right as "only an interest," he said, means that "the sanctity disappears."[88]

According to the Progressives, property is not something that rightfully belongs to the person who earns it; property is whatever the government chooses to recognize as property. The government may adopt protections for property, or abolish those protections, as it pleases. To complain, therefore, about the government's "taking" a person's property is a contradiction in terms. As Brandeis put it, "[I]n the interest of the public and in order to preserve the liberty and the property of the great majority of the citizens of a state, rights of property and the liberty of the individual must be remolded, from time to time, to meet the changing needs of society."[89]

Given that attitude, the Progressives could place no meaningful limits on government authority, since even the most oppressive government action could be described as merely "remolding" the victim's "liberty." Not surprisingly, therefore, the Progressive Era witnessed the birth of intrusive government programs that violated property rights in many ways, as well as other kinds of rights closely related to property rights. Progressives imposed a military draft[90] and censored those who opposed it[91]; implemented eugenics programs, including forced sterilization[92]; and instituted racial segregation,[93] Prohibition,[94] a government monopoly on education,[95] and even requirements that children recite the Pledge of Allegiance.[96] The Progressive Era also saw a vast expansion of government's power of eminent domain. The California Supreme Court held that eminent domain could be used not only for schools, forts, and roads but also for "anything calculated to promote the education, the recreation or the pleasure of the public."[97]

The Progressives also greatly expanded the government's power to dictate the uses of private property. Without even seeking congressional approval, President Theodore Roosevelt designated large areas of land as off limits to development.[98] The federal government dictated business decisions under the antitrust laws, began collecting a new graduated income tax, and opened an array of new bureaucracies to oversee everything from the handling of food and drugs to the money supply. Local authority increased, too; in 1926 the Supreme Court upheld the validity of zoning in *Euclid v. Ambler Realty*,[99] a case that gave the choice of how to use land not to its owner but to the majority of the community,[100] with disastrous implications for racial minorities, who were systematically excluded from neighborhoods.[101] In fact, some scholars argue that zoning laws and policies of "urban renewal" were principally designed to cleanse communities of unwelcome ethnic groups.[102] It was during the Progressive Era that the term "blight" was first used to describe allegedly deteriorating neighborhoods, and although the term was first employed by Progressive sociologist Ernest Burgess as if it were an objective, scientific description, his observations regarding the deterioration of Chicago were neither objective nor scientific. He attributed the "speeding up of the junking process" to the "influx of southern Negroes" into Chicago after World War I.[103] Another study conducted in the 1920s concluded that "certain racial and national groups . . . cause a greater physical deterioration of property than groups higher in the social and economic scale."[104] As Eric Claeys concludes, Progressive Era land-use regulations were often "a polite way of excluding 'undesirable' residents like new immigrants and members of different races."[105]

Their hostility to property rights led some Progressives to severely criticize the Constitution itself.[106] Historian Charles Beard argued that the Constitution was designed to perpetuate class structures, keeping the rich rich and the poor poor, through its protections for private property and economic liberty.[107] Others argued that the document should be reinterpreted to diminish its limits on government power. "The Constitution," wrote Howard Lee McBain, in *The Living Constitution*—a book that marked the first appearance of the term "living Constitution"—was written to serve "not society but the individual." Yet America was "slowly mov[ing] from individualism to collectivism, as move no doubt we must," and that movement would have to be directed by politicians and judges sympathetic to reform efforts.[108] Herbert Croly, whose 1909 book *The Promise of American Life* was popular among the Progressives, was more explicit. Government, he wrote, must

> possess the power of taking any action, which, in the opinion of a decisive majority of the people, is demanded by the public welfare. Such is not the case with the government organized under the Federal Constitution. In respect to certain fundamental provisions, which necessarily receive the most rigid interpretation on the part of the courts, it is practically unmodifiable. A very small percentage of the American people can in this respect permanently thwart the will of an enormous majority, and there can be no justification for such

> a condition. . . . The time may come when the fulfillment of
> a justifiable democratic purpose may demand the limitation
> of certain rights, to which the Constitution affords such abso-
> lute guarantees; and in that case the American democracy
> might be forced to seek by revolutionary means the accom-
> plishment of a result which should be attainable under the
> law.[109]

Despite their complaints that amendment was too difficult, Progressives added more to the Constitution than any generation before
or since: four amendments were passed in only seven years. Those
amendments authorized the direct election of senators, imposed an
income tax, gave women the right to vote, and allowed the federal
government power to prohibit the sale of alcohol.

But amendment was not enough: Progressives also tried to alter
the Constitution's limits through reinterpretation.[110] "We are in these
latter days," wrote Woodrow Wilson, "apt to be very impatient of
literal and dogmatic interpretations of constitutional principle."[111]
A contemporary admirer of Justice Holmes praised him as "too
learned in the history of the law to be blind to the fact that the
socialistic trend in American political thought would finally demand
extensive paternal legislation." But in spite of the evident "necessity
for the establishment of a benevolent attitude towards social
reform," the Constitution prohibited such legislation, and it was
unrealistic to expect any more constitutional amendments. "Next to
amendment of the Constitution, the most feasible means of giving
validity to new principles was to change the interpretation of [its]
provisions," and this Holmes commenced to do, along with allies
such as Brandeis.[112]

Holmes developed the theory of "judicial restraint," arguing that
the role of a judge was extremely limited and that such notions as
"substantive due process" were really just fictions that allowed
judges to impose their own will in the form of legal interpretation.
Instead, Holmes argued, judges should stand back and allow the
will of the majority to prevail. "I always say," Holmes wrote to a
friend, "that if my fellow citizens want to go to Hell I will help
them. It's my job."[113] This view of the judge's role, however, was
unprecedented in American law. According to the Framers of the
Constitution, courts existed to prevent the legislature from exceeding

its proper limits, and this required the judges—as Alexander Hamilton put it—to act as "faithful guardians of the Constitution [even] where legislative invasions of it had been instigated by the major voice of the community."[114] Yet according to Holmes, the majority should be free to do almost anything it might wish. In most cases, Holmes explained, "the word 'liberty' . . . is perverted when it is held to prevent the natural outcome of a dominant opinion."[115]

Holmes professed not to have an opinion about *what* the majority chose to do; he just defended its authority to do what it pleased. Brandeis, on the other hand, actively argued in favor of limits on free enterprise and private property rights, even after he was placed on the Supreme Court. In case after case, he defended Progressive laws that "remolded" the property rights of individuals. States, he argued, should act as laboratories, performing experiments on human subjects even if those experiments deprived citizens of their right to own property and to earn a living.[116] The combination of Holmes's theory of judicial restraint and Brandeis's theory of activist government laid the groundwork for the constitutional revolution that came during the New Deal.[117]

The New Deal Paradigm

The Progressive assault on property rights did not succeed overnight. The election of Calvin Coolidge and other events delayed the government's campaign against private property. But with the coming of the New Deal, the Progressives triumphed at last. The New Deal brought an unprecedented expansion of government control over the economy, redistributing property and benefits in ways that government officials considered most socially beneficial. The New Deal's leaders regarded property solely as a creation of the state, and the state could seize it, change the rules governing it, or transfer it between citizens virtually at will. Property, wrote a contemporary observer, "is itself a highly collectivistic institution, dependent for its existence upon very substantial restraints . . . upon individual freedom. At any given period of time, therefore, the law intervenes, not only to protect individual owners . . . but also to safeguard individuals and the community as a whole against oppressive and incompetent uses of property."[118] That authority was not limited to preventing people from hurting one another; it included the authority to dictate how much a person could own and what a person could do with his property.

By confusing governmental *protection* of private property with governmental *creation* of property, the New Dealers rationalized increasing government interference with the belongings of private citizens. Political thinkers began to emphasize democracy rather than liberty as the basic principle of American government—focusing on the ability of majorities to enact their preferences into law, rather than the freedom of individuals to pursue happiness and keep the fruits of their labors. In 1940 a leading Progressive lawyer, Roscoe Pound, expressed some hesitation about the path that he had helped political theory to take. "Americans of the last century held that democracy was to achieve a regime of ideal individual liberty and to do it by leaving everyone as free as possible to find and take advantage of opportunity," he wrote. But now "they seem to hold that democracy is to achieve an ideal regime of security by providing everyone not with opportunity but with a guaranteed minimum of the material goods of existence, and that this end is to be achieved by administrative regulation of every form of individual activity . . . [by] some presumably expert agency of government."[119] The result was a tendency toward government absolutism in which there was "no real check on [government's] rule-making power." Americans were living "under a regime of arbitrary official action" that was similar to the tyrannies that the Founders had rebelled against.[120] The Progressives had established the principle that individual rights were merely permissions.

Yet, as the administrative state expanded, it ran up against more and more constitutional problems. The New Dealers faced the difficult task of creating a government that the Framers of the Constitution had never anticipated—indeed, had guarded against. To justify increasing interference with private property and economic freedom required a major reinterpretation of the Constitution, along the lines that Holmes and Brandeis had proposed. Irving Brant, a prominent New Deal intellectual, argued that lawyers and politicians faced a "fundamental necessity" to "find power through which federal and state governments . . . may cope with the economic and social problems of the twentieth century." Brant proposed three ways to find such power: amending the Constitution, restricting the power of judicial review, or packing the Supreme Court with "liberal" justices.[121] But Brant rejected the Court-packing plan as too dangerous and the proposal to amend the Constitution as too burdensome; it was "hopeless to think of a general amendment," he concluded.[122] The only path was to change how the Constitution was interpreted and transform the Supreme Court into "a weapon of social and economic reform."[123]

That reinterpretation came in 1934 with *Nebbia v. New York*.[124] In that case the Court considered the constitutionality of a state law that prohibited people from selling milk at low prices. The law was intended to protect some dairies against competition from others, a policy that increased the price of milk to the consumer and thus did not benefit the public—it violated the generality requirement of the Due Process Clause. But in *Nebbia,* the Court all but eliminated the generality requirement. Instead, it invented a new "rational basis" test, under which a law would be declared constitutional so long as it was "rationally related to a legitimate government interest," a test that almost any law could pass. The *Nebbia* decision vastly expanded the power of states to regulate private behavior: what lawyers refer to as the state's "police power." States are "free to adopt whatever economic policy may reasonably be deemed to promote public welfare," wrote Justice Owen Roberts for the Court. Any intervention into economic transactions that could be "seen to have a reasonable relation to a proper legislative purpose" would satisfy the Due Process Clause.[125]

But by "reasonable," the Court did not mean that a law must actually be sensible or that it accomplish the legislature's goals. In fact, even a law that could not possibly accomplish its stated goal could still be upheld as constitutional.[126] Three years later the Court held that more stringent tests would be applied to laws that interfered with certain preferred freedoms, but to this day *Nebbia*'s "rational basis test" remains the test applied whenever a person claims that the state is violating property rights, or other disfavored rights. Holmes's theory of "judicial restraint" has triumphed at last.

Throughout the decades that followed, the Court's deference to the legislative power expanded into the field of employment contracts,[127] eminent domain,[128] and even the Contracts Clause.[129] In *Home Building & Loan Assn. v. Blaisdell,* for example, the Supreme Court allowed Minnesota to force landlords to continue renting property to tenants who had not paid their rent, unilaterally rewriting countless lease contracts in the state. Although the Constitution forbids states from making laws that impair the obligations of contract, the Court declared that the Depression was an "emergency" that the Constitution's authors could not have foreseen and that "the economic interests of the state may justify the exercise of its continuing and dominant protective power notwithstanding interference with contracts."[130]

Twenty years after *Nebbia*, the Court considered the power of eminent domain in *Berman v. Parker*,[131] a case involving an urban renewal project in Washington, D.C. City bureaucrats decided to condemn 15 square blocks of the city[132] (97.5 percent of which were black-owned property)[133] in an effort to "clean up" the neighborhood. Among the properties seized was a department store owned by Max Morris. The store was not a slum; in fact, it was condemned solely because it was in the same neighborhood as a slum. Nor did the government contend that the land would be used by the government. Rather, the plan involved transferring Morris's property to another retailer to operate a store for private profit. Morris sued, contending that the Constitution allowed the government to use eminent domain only "for public use" not for private use. The Court ruled unanimously against him. Justice William O. Douglas, a Franklin Roosevelt appointee, held that government's responsibility includes the power to maintain not only "public safety, public health, morality, peace and quiet, law and order" but also the power to combat "miserable and disreputable housing conditions," to maintain "the spirit [of the people]," and to eliminate "ugly" property in the community.[134] It was up to the legislature to decide what projects to undertake: "[W]hen the legislature has spoken, the public interest has been declared in terms well-nigh conclusive." Thus, if the legislature decide that the public would be "better served" if a piece of property were given to someone else, the courts "cannot say" that such a redistribution is unconstitutional.[135]

Douglas's heavy emphasis on the legislature's discretion was simply a rephrasing of the theory behind *Nebbia*. The earlier case had expanded the government's power to control the economic relationships between people by holding that laws governing economic affairs need only be "rationally related to a legitimate government interest." In *Berman*, Douglas used that same lax standard to declare that government could seize land outright and transfer it to those individuals or groups it preferred.[136] After *Nebbia*, the government could (to use Brandeis's word) "remold" the freedom of contract in whatever way it found preferable; after *Berman,* the state could "remold" the rights of property in the same way. In fact, as one federal court noted 15 years after *Berman* was decided, "the whole scheme" in economic redevelopment cases "is for a public agency to take one man's property away from him and sell it to another." That was hardly what the Founding Fathers had had in mind, "but the process has been upheld uniformly by latter-day judicial decision. . . . [U]nder all modern federal decisions our hands are tied—if the book on the procedure is followed."[137]

While the Court was giving government greater power to seize private property, it was also giving the government greater power to legislate how landowners could use their property. As early as 1871 the Supreme Court held that the government must pay property owners when it forbids them from using their land, just as it does when it actually takes title to land through eminent domain.[138] That idea, which has come to be called the theory of "regulatory takings," forbids the government from exploiting a dangerous loophole: if government could forbid people to use their property without compensating them on the grounds that it hadn't physically seized the land, then government would simply order people to use their property in various ways, leave them technically in possession, and never have to pay just compensation. But the right to private property is, after all, simply the right to *use* property. If the government takes away the *use* of property, then it has "taken" an important part of it away from the owner and should have to pay compensation. As Justice Holmes put it, "[W]hile property may be regulated to a certain extent, if regulation goes too far it will be recognized as a taking."[139]

Unfortunately, the Supreme Court has never said at what point a law "goes too far" and requires compensation. In 1979 the owners of New York's historic Penn Central railroad station sued for compensation when the city prohibited them from constructing an office tower on their land. This regulation, they argued, "went too far" and was a taking. But the Supreme Court disagreed.[140] The just compensation requirement had to yield to government's authority to "adjust[] the benefits and burdens of economic life,"[141] wrote Justice William Brennan. Instead of examining whether government ought to be in the business of such "adjustments" in the first place, Brennan simply took it for granted that government could redistribute the property of citizens.

The *Penn Central* case did not entirely abandon the concept of regulatory takings. Instead, it devised a "test" for courts to use for determining when a regulation reached the level of a taking. Shunning clear, strict rules, the new "test" would allow courts to employ "essentially ad hoc, factual inquiries" when considering such factors as "the extent to which the regulation has interfered with distinct investment-backed expectations" and "the character of the governmental action."[142]

The *Penn Central* test, which remains in place today, has none of the rigor of a genuine legal test. In fact, it is essentially inscrutable. It allows the courts to base decisions on an unpredictable framework of highly subjective considerations. In fact, it is essentially inscrutable. Only a year after the *Penn Central* test was created, the Supreme Court changed it: the courts were to assess not simply a law's interference with "investment-backed expectations" but also whether those expectations were "reasonable" to begin with.[143] If a court finds that an owner's intent to use his property is not "reasonable," then compensation is not required. And the "reasonableness" of those expectations depends mostly on whether the judges think the government's interference is "fair." With the compensation requirement diluted to such a degree, it is hardly surprising that the Supreme Court has never compensated a property owner under the *Penn Central* test. The test erects an illusion of lawfulness in an atmosphere in which government may impose the most arbitrary and burdensome limits on the rights of a property owner.[144]

During the 1980s there was reason to hope that the Supreme Court would change its course and pay more attention to protecting people from regulations that deprived them of the value of their property. Beginning in 1982 with *Loretto v. Teleprompter Manhattan CATV Corp.*,[145] the Supreme Court began to give the issue more serious consideration than it had in its confused *Penn Central* decision. In *Loretto* the Court found that a law requiring landlords to install cable television on their property required compensation because it forced an owner to let people or things onto her land without her consent. "The power to exclude has traditionally been considered one of the most treasured strands in an owner's bundle of property rights," wrote Justice Thurgood Marshall, and the cable television requirement violated that by forcing the owner to place a one-inch cable on her building.[146]

A few years later, in *Nollan v. California Coastal Commission*,[147] the Court found that a family's rights were violated when the state required them to provide public access across their property in exchange for a building permit. The California Coastal Commission was essentially demanding that the Nollans give away some of their land, not as part of a program to protect the public from some harmful use of the property, but simply to enrich the public at the Nollans' expense. Such an "out-and-out plan of extortion," wrote Justice Antonin Scalia, was not a legitimate use of the government's power.[148] Rather, when government required a property owner to meet certain conditions in exchange for a building permit, those conditions had to have something to do with the effect that the construction would actually have on the neighborhood. It might be constitutional, for example, for a city to require a person proposing to build a new shopping center to pay a fee to widen the streets to handle the increased traffic, but it would not be reasonable to require a property owner building a single-family home to widen the streets. Moreover, wrote Justice Scalia, regulations limiting the use of land were required to meet a higher standard than the "rationally related" standard that the Court had applied to economic regulations ever since *Nebbia*.[149] Then, in *Dolan v. City of Tigard*,[150] the Court elaborated on its *Nollan* decision: not only do building permit conditions have to have some connection to the consequences of a new development, but the condition must be "roughly proportional" to those consequences, meaning that the government may not demand an exorbitant fee for a minor impact. And in *Lucas v. South Carolina Coastal Commission*,[151] the Court found that when regulations deprive property owners of the full value of their property, compensation is due just as if the property had actually been seized.

Although those and similar cases during the 1980s and 1990s caused many people to hope that the Court had rediscovered the importance of property rights,[152] that hope would prove to be unwarranted. At the beginning of the 21st century, the Court once again turned its back on this cornerstone of liberty.

4. The State of Property Rights Today

When Dorothy English and her husband Nykee bought 39 acres of land near Portland, Oregon, in 1953, they thought it would not only help provide them with retirement income but would also help them provide for their children's future.[1] Over the next 10 years, they built their dream home while they lived in a run-down house that didn't even have plumbing, and they sold half of the land to support the family. But in 1973 the Oregon legislature enacted SB 100, one of the most restrictive land-use regulation schemes in the nation. Shortly afterwards, county officials acting under the statute declared the Englishes' remaining property "forest land" and prohibited them from subdividing their property into anything smaller than 20-acre plots. Dorothy's wish to leave investment property to her children and grandchildren vanished with the stroke of a bureaucrat's pen.

Dorothy didn't object to environmental protection laws, but the new ordinance destroyed thousands of dollars of value that she and her husband had rightfully earned. Under the Constitution, government is required to compensate people whenever it takes their property for public use. "Who's supposed to pay for all this [forest] they want to save?" Dorothy asked a reporter. "If the majority wants to save this stuff, then the majority should pay for it."[2] But under the decisions of Oregon courts, government almost never has to pay for property as long as it doesn't take *title* to the land.[3] Rather than condemn land outright, therefore, Oregon officials simply order property owners not to do anything with their land— except pay the taxes, insurance, and other such bills.

Regulatory Takings

Dorothy's case typifies the burdens imposed on homeowners by state and federal land-use regulations. Those burdens grew throughout the latter half of the 20th century, largely as a result of cases like *Penn Central*, which decreased the government's obligation to compensate property owners. At about the time those cases were being decided, the Johnson and Nixon administrations were implementing some of the most extensive government controls on property in the nation's history. In 1974 Sen. Henry M. Jackson of Washington proposed a national land-use planning act that would have given federal authorities the power to grant or deny building permits throughout the country.[4] Although the bill was approved by the Senate, it failed in the House of Representatives, in part because such issues had always been considered a local affair. But shortly thereafter, a series of environmental regulations that did pass accomplished something very similar. The Clean Air Act, the Clean Water Act, the National Environmental Policy Act, and the Endangered Species Act created layers of federal bureaucracy with power over land use whenever such use might adversely affect the environment in even the most infinitesimal way.

Those laws were written in extraordinarily broad terms to ensure that the government would have the maximum possible authority. For example, the Clean Water Act made it a federal crime to "discharge a pollutant" into a "water of the United States," but a "pollutant" came to be defined as absolutely anything, including sand, fish, and even sunlight.[5] In the 1970s Sen. Edmund S. Muskie, one of the authors of the Clean Water Act, boasted that mixing scotch and water in a glass would violate the law.[6] From a legal standpoint, that is almost literally true, because not only is a "pollutant" defined as absolutely anything, but a "water of the United States" has come to mean more than just lakes, rivers, and streams. It now means any body of water from which a single molecule of water can travel to a major river, even if it takes a very long, indirect route.[7] That is referred to as "hydrological connection," and under this theory federal bureaucrats may regulate any body of water—and land next to it—even if the "hydrological connection" is only intermittent and extremely minor. There is no legal reason why a bathtub or a kitchen sink—or even a glass of scotch and water—could not qualify as a "water of the United States." In fact, in one case in 1985, a federal appeals court held that the federal government had regulatory authority when a company's pollutants were poured into a small arroyo that never connected to a significant river but "soak[ed] into the earth's surface, bec[a]me part of the underground aquifers, and after a lengthy period, *perhaps centuries,* the underground water moves toward eventual discharge at Horace Springs or the Rio San Jose."[8]

What's more, even perfectly dry land can qualify as a "wetland" under the Clean Water Act, even when situated many miles from the nearest waterway.[9] As an Army Corps of Engineers official once boasted, "For regulatory purposes, a wetland is whatever we decide it is."[10] In one case in 2003, real estate developer John Rapanos was sentenced to federal prison for moving sand from one spot to another on a Michigan cornfield located 20 miles from the nearest waterway.[11] Likewise, the Endangered Species Act requires a federal permit for any development that might in any way affect an animal or plant on the list of endangered species. But because the list is so long, virtually any development can require the approval of federal bureaucrats—approval that can take years or even decades and tens or hundreds of thousands of dollars. Violations of environmental laws, of course, carry extremely severe civil and criminal penalties.

The expansion of administrative control by federal, state, and local government has led to a de facto reversal of the old principle of private property. Before the Progressive Era, a property owner was presumed to have the right to do with his property whatever he pleased so long as he respected the rights of others to enjoy their property. Obviously, if a person set a fire on his land and the smoke interfered significantly with his neighbor's ability to use and enjoy her land, he would be liable for committing a nuisance. But in most other respects property owners were at liberty to use their property as they wished. The common law developed a phrase, *sic utere tuo ut alienum non laedas*, meaning "use what is yours so as not to harm what belongs to others." If a neighbor (or government) wanted to stop a person from using his land, the neighbor had to give a good reason for doing so. But in today's administrative state, an owner is generally presumed *not* to have the right to use his land: he must ask for permission from a government agency, and permits can be denied for practically any reason and delayed for virtually any length of time.[12] Property is thus effectively enjoyed at the pleasure of the government, which grants or withholds permission to use it—or revokes ownership entirely, through eminent domain—depending on political considerations.

State authority to control the use of land grew alongside the power of the federal government. Oregon's SB 100 and laws like it imposed increasing costs on property owners, forbidding them to use their property for things they had long planned. For 20 years after the state declared her property "forest land," Dorothy English was forbidden to subdivide it and give it to her children. Although the Oregon legislature passed a special bill to allow her to divide her property, the governor vetoed it, citing the importance of fully enforcing the state's land-use laws. Finally, in 2000 frustrated Oregonians passed a statewide ballot initiative that required government to pay people like Dorothy for the value taken from them through regulations. Although the law did not apply to government's power to prevent environmental destruction or traditional nuisances, the measure was still attacked by environmental groups and others who want government to have as much authority as possible over private property. Those opposition groups outspent the initiative's proponents by a factor of three to one, and nearly every newspaper in the state editorialized against it. But Measure 7 passed anyway, adding some of the strongest property protections in the nation to the state constitution. Shortly after it passed, however, it was challenged in court by several environmental groups, and the state supreme court held it unconstitutional. One provision in the measure held that laws against pornography shops were not the kinds of regulations that required compensation; the court seized on that provision, declaring that it violated the freedom of speech.[13]

Oregon's voters reacted to this decision with anger, and in 2004 they passed an almost identical measure, called Measure 37. Again, the opposition was intense; once more it outspent proponents by a factor of three to one; and again virtually all newspapers opposed it. But Measure 37 passed by a margin of three to two, receiving more "yes" votes than any initiative in Oregon history. After three decades, Dorothy English finally had the opportunity to fulfill her promise to herself and her family—to divide her land and give it to her children and grandchildren, or receive compensation for her losses.[14] In February 2006 the Oregon Supreme Court ruled that Measure 37 is constitutional.[15]

One reason pro-regulation forces argue that government should not have to compensate property owners for the burdens of regulation is that they confuse two fundamentally different kinds of laws: laws that protect individual rights and laws that provide society with what economists call "public goods."[16] Laws protecting individual

82

rights—enacted under the government's "police powers"—may cause losses to those they restrict, but the government doesn't have to pay for those losses because the activities restricted were wrong to begin with. Government doesn't have to compensate people when it prohibits them from polluting their neighbors' property, for example, because it isn't taking away anything they had the right to do in the first place. But laws that force property owners to provide the public with things the public would otherwise have to buy— such as parks or wildlife habitat—are a different matter. Those laws are designed not to protect rights but to provide the public with goods. When the costs of providing such goods fall on a single person or a small group, the public needs to compensate those owners for their losses. Unless the owner is compensated by the regulation itself—which sometimes happens through an increase in the value of an affected property—the owner ends up paying the full costs of the public good.[17]

There are an enormous number of regulatory schemes that force individual landowners to bear the cost of providing public benefits. Often the result is harmful, not just to the owner, but also to the supposed beneficiaries of those programs. One especially sad example is "rent control," which prohibits landlords from charging their tenants what they could get for an apartment if the landlord and tenants were free to decide the terms of their own contracts. Rent control laws are often passed by people who believe that they protect the poor and the elderly from poverty and homelessness, but in fact they end up hurting those people most of all.

Controls on rents have the same perverse consequences that other price controls have. They disrupt the normal coordination of supply and demand that takes place in the free market, decreasing the incentives for property owners to provide rental housing and limiting the choices available to those wishing to rent. Providers of housing are less likely to invest in new apartment buildings or to maintain their existing stock. When landlords' losses mount, some convert their rental units into condominiums that can be sold for a market price. In some cases, government has even tried to close off that avenue of escape by making it illegal for landlords to get out of the business. In 1984 the California Supreme Court upheld the constitutionality of a Santa Monica ordinance forbidding owners of rental property from "remov[ing] a controlled rental unit from the rental housing market by demolition, conversion or other means."[18] The court declared that the law imposed only an "indirect and minimal burden" on the landowners' "asserted liberty interest."[19] Fortunately, the state legislature later passed a law allowing landlords to get out of the business if they wanted to, but the decision itself has never been overruled. If landlords can't or don't want to stop providing rental housing to the public, limitations on what they may charge mean that they must cut costs as much as possible, which often means they won't repair broken pipes, paint hallways, or otherwise keep their property up to code. Sometimes they abandon the property altogether. Ultimately, rent control makes it harder for a poor person to find a place to rent and more likely that the apartment he does find will be substandard. Meanwhile, one coercive intrusion into voluntary exchange is piled on the last, and freedom is further restricted.

Although some existing tenants benefit from rent control by paying cheaper rents, they do so only at the expense of property owners—and those who are still searching for places to live. As economist George Reisman puts it:

> The tenant who is able to afford a better car, say, or an extra vacation, because of the artificially low rent he pays, is buying that car or vacation at the expense of part of a new apartment building somewhere, and ultimately he is buying it at the expense of the upkeep of the very building in which he lives. The day comes when he wants to move and finds no decent place to move to, because he and millions of others like him have consumed the equivalent of all the new apartment buildings that should have been built.[20]

Rent control also creates a black market for artificially cheap housing, as potential renters—often wealthy or middle class—scramble to find rent-controlled apartments, sometimes by bribing landlords to take them on as tenants. Sometimes tenants in rent-controlled apartments sublet their apartments to other people, charging enough to pay the owner and still make a profit. Rarely will a poor person, new to the neighborhood or lacking a credit history, prevail in such a competition.

Even though economists agree almost universally that rent control does not help the poor, some cities continue to enforce those laws, because voters often do not realize the harms they cause and because rent control, like many environmental laws, allows politicians to avoid raising taxes. Rent control provides low-cost housing without the government having to pay for it; instead, the cost is borne by the landlord. The public at large rarely realizes how much such programs actually cost. As Justice Scalia explained in a rent control case, regulations that impose costs on property owners are attractive to politicians because they "permit[] wealth transfers . . . to be achieved 'off budget,' with relative invisibility and thus relative immunity from normal democratic processes." A city might help poor renters by simply raising the city's taxes and using that money to pay part of their rent. But doing so would cause the public to pay more attention, and voters might disapprove of programs that often benefit middle-class renters rather than the poor. "It seems to me doubtful," Scalia continued, "whether the citizens of San Jose would allow funds in the municipal treasury, from wherever derived, to be distributed to a family of four with income as high as $32,400 a year. . . . The voters might well see other, more pressing, social priorities."[21]

In case after case, environmental laws, rent control, scenic regulations, historic preservation ordinances, architectural design review, building permit limitations, and countless other regulations confiscate some of the wealth that property owners have in their land— wealth they have acquired by working hard, saving, and investing in property to provide for their future and build their dreams—and transfer that wealth to the general public or to private interest groups. Rarely, if ever, are these people justly compensated for what the government takes from them. But public projects are supposed to be paid for by taxes levied on the public, because the public enjoys the benefits. Just as it would be unfair to require one person in a city to build a public park or to underwrite the entire budget of the city's police department, so it is unjust to allow politicians to shift the cost of public projects onto small groups of politically powerless individuals, such as landlords or real estate developers, and thus to provide the public with "free" benefits.

Not only is this unfair to the person or group singled out to pay the costs, it also reduces the accountability of politicians by allowing them to avoid difficult aspects of the democratic process. Outright condemnation of property is usually well publicized; the public learns about it through newspapers and television and can deliberate about the costs and benefits of the proposal. But imposing severe regulatory costs on a particular homeowner or business is much less visible; as the New York Court of Appeals put it:

> The ultimate evil of a deprivation of property, or better, a frustration of property rights, under the guise of an exercise of the police power is that it forces the owner to assume the cost of providing a benefit to the public without recoupment. There is no attempt to share the cost of the benefit among those benefited, that is, society at large. Instead, the accident of ownership determines who shall bear the cost initially. Of course, as further consequence, the ultimate economic cost of providing the benefit is hidden from those who in a democratic society are given the power of deciding whether or not they wish to obtain the benefit despite the ultimate economic cost, however initially distributed. In other words, the removal from productive use of private property has an ultimate social cost more easily concealed by imposing the cost on the owner alone. When successfully concealed, the public is not likely to have any objection to the "cost-free" benefit.[22]

Preventing the government from imposing the costs of its programs on particular individuals would promote a healthier democratic process. It would ensure more rational and open decisionmaking because the public could more clearly weigh the costs and benefits of government programs.

The Supreme Court seemed to recognize this principle in *Owen v. City of Independence*[23] when it held that cities could be forced to pay damages for violating citizens' civil rights. "The knowledge that a municipality will be liable for all of its injurious conduct, whether committed in good faith or not, should create an incentive for officials . . . to err on the side of protecting citizens' constitutional rights," wrote Justice Brennan. Since "it is the public at large which enjoys the benefits of the government's activities, and it is the public at large which is ultimately responsible for its administration," it is "fairer to allocate any resulting financial loss to the inevitable costs of government borne by all the taxpayers, than to allow its impact to be felt solely by those whose rights . . . have been violated."[24] If providing an incentive to make well-informed decisions is a proper goal of civil rights laws—and it certainly is—then it should also be a goal of the just compensation requirement.

Of course, many of the costs of regulation are eventually borne by the public in one way or another. Regulations that make business more expensive and risky drive up the costs of providing goods and services, push some producers out of business, and restrict supply so much that some products are simply no longer available at all.[25] In California, for example, the median price of a house increased more than 12.5 percent in a single year, reaching more than $509,000 in May 2005.[26] In some California counties, the cost of new homes increased by more than 60 percent in three years. Yet as the price of homes exploded, the cost of the labor and materials that go into constructing them did not increase significantly. Nor were developers simply increasing their profits. Instead, the single largest reason for the high cost of a home is the price of permission to build.[27] The cost—and the delay—of getting permits is so high that, as economists John M. Quigley and Steven Raphael of the University of California at Berkeley recently concluded, "[C]ities with the greatest increase in housing demand experienced the lowest increases in new housing supply."[28] Land-use regulations are making it harder every day for anyone but the super-rich to find homes.

Although in the 1980s cases such as *Lucas* and *Loretto* gave property owners some hope that courts would begin taking the problem of regulatory takings more seriously, that hope has recently been set back by a series of Supreme Court decisions letting government off the hook for the costs it imposes on citizens. Avoiding the relatively clear lines set down in *Lucas* and *Loretto*, courts gradually discovered ways to use the malleable *Penn Central* test instead, meaning that the property owner nearly always loses his case.

Even when courts did apply the *Lucas* or *Loretto* rulings, they used a variety of logical tricks to avoid compensating property owners. *Lucas*, for example, holds that government must pay just compensation whenever its laws deprive a person of *all* of the value of a piece of property. But suppose the government takes all but a tiny portion of that property—say, by allowing a person who owns 10 acres to use only 10 percent of his land. According to one interpretation, the owner must be paid the full value of nine acres, since the government is depriving him of *all value* of those nine acres. But according to another interpretation, the owner is not due any compensation at all. Because he is still allowed *some use* of the land, the government's action is not considered a taking to begin with. Lawyers call this discrepancy the

87

"relevant parcel" or "denominator" problem, and it allows courts to declare that no taking has occurred at all if the government allows an owner to use some small fraction of the property. In one recent case, the government of Rhode Island prohibited a landowner from doing anything with his land, which was probably worth as much as $3 million, except to build a single house valued at $200,000 at most.[29] By allowing the owner to keep this token value, the state escaped having to compensate him.

The Supreme Court dealt a far more serious blow to property rights in the *Tahoe-Sierra* case in 2002. In that case, Justice Stevens declared that the government would not have to pay property owners for banning all construction in the Lake Tahoe area for more than 20 years through a series of supposedly "temporary" prohibitions. Since government cannot afford to pay for all of the value it takes from people, it is not required to pay at all: "A rule that required compensation for every delay in the use of property would render routine government processes prohibitively expensive or encourage hasty decisionmaking."[30] Then, in 2005 the Court took another step, holding that even when a land-use regulation cannot possibly accomplish the goal it is supposed to accomplish, government is not required to pay just compensation.[31] Cases since the 1980s had suggested that laws that cannot accomplish their ostensible aim "go too far" and therefore require compensation, but now the Court has explained that such laws are subject only to the lax "rational relationship" standard invented in *Nebbia*, meaning, once again, that the property owner will virtually always lose.

State courts became even more hostile to people seeking compensation for the costs of regulations after 1980. Perhaps the most egregious example of bureaucrats imposing severe costs on particular property owners is the case of the historic San Remo Hotel in San Francisco.[32] Many of the city's hotels had for years rented out rooms on a long-term basis instead of catering to tourists night by night. But as the tourism industry in San Francisco improved, some of those hotels decided they could make more money by switching to nightly rentals. That's when city officials, claiming that the city's housing shortage would worsen if residential hotels were allowed to rent to tourists, passed the Hotel Conversion Ordinance. The ordinance required hotel owners to obtain special permits before they could change from residential to tourist service. Even though the San Remo was not actually a residential hotel to begin with, city officials still demanded that the owners get a permit before renting out any more rooms to tourists—a permit that cost the owners of the San Remo more than half a million dollars.[33] The city claimed it would spend this money to construct housing units "equivalent" to the rooms that would now be rented out.[34]

The hotel's owners sued: the regulation violated their rights by essentially forcing them, and them alone, to pay a special tax to care for the city's homeless problem—a problem they had not caused. But the California Supreme Court upheld the law, declaring that it was merely a "burden placed broadly and nondiscriminatorily on changes in property's use."[35] Using the "rational relationship" standard, the court declared that "the housing replacement fees bear a reasonable relationship to loss of housing" caused by a hotel's conversion to tourist use and that the property owner's rights had therefore not been violated. Indeed, the court even declared that requiring the city to compensate property owners for the infringement of their property rights would be imposing a "personal theory of political economy . . . on the people of a democratic state"![36]

Of course, the whole point of property rights is to prevent "the people" from "democratically" choosing to take away the rights of a minority. As Justice Janice Rogers Brown explained in her dissenting opinion, the Hotel Conversion Ordinance "affect[ed] a relatively powerless group" merely because they were powerless.[37] Describing the ordinance as a kind of extortion racket, Brown explained that the city was essentially using its police power as a fundraising tool. First it banned owners from using their property as they wished

> and then [raised income by] selling exemptions from the regulatory scheme. . . . The government, in effect, says: We have the power; therefore, pay us to leave you alone. . . . Instead of the government having to pay compensation to property owners, the government now wants property owners to compensate it to get back the fair value of property the government took away through regulation.[38]

After the state courts upheld the law, the federal courts refused to intervene and the Hotel Conversion Ordinance was allowed to remain.[39]

Regulatory takings are increasingly common today, because court decisions have allowed government to provide "free" goods to the public by imposing the costs "off budget" on individual property owners. This allows bureaucrats to live by different rules than those that apply to the rest of us. People's desires may be infinite, but their resources are not. Responsible people must therefore set priorities and make choices to stay within their budgets. But government has found a way to provide values to people—everything from scenic forest views to shelters for the homeless—without having to pay for them. By not enforcing the just compensation requirement, courts have allowed private interest groups to grant themselves benefits without requiring politically unpopular tax increases. And many of those courts, including California's, have rationalized that refusal by saying that requiring compensation would undermine democratic decisionmaking. In reality, requiring compensation would enhance democratic decisionmaking, because voters and politicians would make rational choices among alternatives, and because those who get the benefits would also bear some of the costs. In the end, of course, the "free" government benefits provided by regulatory takings are not free. They are paid for by individual property owners—people like Dorothy English.

Eminent Domain

Regulatory takings deprive owners of the right to use their property but allow them to keep title to the land. But under the power of eminent domain, government seizes the property outright. Eminent domain was once regarded as "a very high and dangerous" power that government should rarely use,[40] but the last half of the 20th century saw government increasingly willing to wield its authority to force people to relinquish their property to the government. *Berman v. Parker* was only one of many decisions handed down in the 1950s that expanded this power; courts in California,[41] Ohio,[42] Massachusetts,[43] and several other states also broadened the power to condemn homes and businesses for "redevelopment" projects.

Those projects were devised by urban planners who believed that it is the government's role to intervene and improve the economy by subsidizing businesses or by transferring land from people who have it to others who will put it to more economically productive uses. According to that theory, businesses that might create jobs or boost a city's economy are often unable to do so because property owners refuse to sell their land except at exorbitant prices. Such

90

"holdout" property owners are able to prevent economic growth, even when everyone else in the neighborhood is willing to sell. Therefore, the theory continues, eminent domain is the proper way to solve the "holdout" problem by forcing the resistant owner to sell at a "reasonable" price.

But in fact the holdout problem is greatly exaggerated. There are many examples of major development projects that have succeeded without the use of eminent domain, despite the alleged danger of holdouts. Disneyland, for example, and highways such as Virginia's Dulles Greenway and the 91 freeway in Southern California, were built without the use of eminent domain, even though landowners could have held out.[44] One reason that projects like those succeed is that property owners often have powerful incentives to sell their land for reasonable prices—for example, many landowners find that if they sell a part of their property, the value of the land they retain is increased. And in many other sectors of the economy, private businesses buy large parcels of land in ways that minimize holdout problems, including blind auctions or other collective-bidding schemes. The sad fact is that redevelopment bureaucrats often accuse property owners of holding out whenever the owners want more than the lowball figure offered by the government.

True holdouts—people who absolutely refuse to sell their land for any price at all—are rare. And even when they do exist, developers are often able to work around them. When 97-year-old Ramon Rodriguez, a resident of the Little Mexico neighborhood of Dallas, refused to sell his land to Frost Bank, the bank's owners simply built their drive-through around him. Until his death in 2004, Rodriguez would sit on his porch and wave at customers and the bank's employees. "The bank people were especially nice to him," his daughter recalls. "And the police would come by and sit with him. We had the privilege of having him a long time."[45] In a way, all property owners are holdouts because they have decided that they would rather keep their land than sell it to someone else that day. The right to hold out is part of what it means to enjoy property rights.

Not only do government officials exaggerate the holdout problem, they also exaggerate the benefits that their projects will bring to communities. That was certainly true of one of the most infamous eminent domain cases of all time: Detroit's decision in 1981 to condemn the Poletown neighborhood and transfer it to General Motors to build a car factory.[46] Contending that the unemployment caused by a severe recession would be alleviated by encouraging GM to open a plant in the area, Detroit officials condemned 465 acres of the working-class neighborhood and transferred them to the country's largest automaker. The case proceeded at an astonishing speed. Less than a year after GM produced its plans, the city had given approval, condemned the property, and won a major victory in the Michigan Supreme Court, which declared that economic development was a "public use" that could be served by seizing the neighborhood through eminent domain. After evicting Poletown's 4,200 residents, GM constructed its plant, which opened in 1984. But it never employed the 6,000 people that the company claimed it would; after several layoffs and restarts, the factory ended up employing only about 2,500 people,[47] and by destroying some 600 businesses, the project probably threw an equal number of people out of work.[48] Like many redevelopment schemes, the Poletown project probably ended up hurting the economy in the long run.

The legal justification for the *Poletown* decision was typical of other cases that allowed, and still allow, government to use eminent domain for economic revitalization. "Public use," the court explained, meant "accomplishing some public good," nothing more.[49] And in any case, "the benefit to be received by the municipality" by keeping GM in the area was "clear and significant." Reducing unemployment and "revitalizing the economic base of the community" were "essential public purposes." In fact, the court held that "the benefit to [GM] is merely incidental" to those goals.[50] Once again, the court never explained why the government has any business controlling the community's "economic base" in the first place.

The court pointed out that many 19th-century cases had allowed the condemnation of land to construct railroads, even though the railroads were operated by private, for-profit corporations. The transfer to GM, said the *Poletown* court, was just another example of that sort of economic progress. But those cases were different in some important ways. Most significant, courts that permitted the condemnation of property for for-profit, private companies had scrupulously attached conditions to the private companies' exploitation of government power. Those conditions were intended to ensure that eminent domain did not get out of hand. For example, the government regulated the prices charged by railroads and mills to ensure that the companies were not unfairly profiting from government favoritism. Richard Epstein has put this in economic terms: condemning land for a development project transfers a value to the recipient of the land that the recipient did not pay for—an economic "surplus" consisting of the difference between the value the recipient gets and the amount the recipient would have had to pay for the land in a voluntary transaction. Without the public use clause, the recipient is able to pocket this difference—to get land below the market price. The Public Use Clause "ensures the 'fair' allocation of [this] surplus by preventing any group from appropriating more than a *pro rata* share" of this difference. That makes sense because eminent domain is a public power, and it should not be used to give special advantages to a private few.[51]

Also, 19th-century courts held that railroads and mills were not allowed to refuse service to any customer. They were therefore public utilities, like power companies today—quasi-governmental entities forced to serve all on a nondiscriminatory basis and at regulated rates of return. Although those justifications were not always convincing, they at least placed a limit on government's power to grant political favors to particular commercial enterprises. General Motors' new Poletown plant had none of those characteristics. It was operated by a private corporation for private profit; GM was not required to allow any member of the public onto the property, nor were its profits regulated by a government board. The new plant simply allowed GM to profit by employing the government's coercive force for its own benefit.

Moreover, courts in the railroad cases had held that trains were really just modern versions of roads, which government had long been in the business of constructing. There was no reason, according to those courts, that the government could not delegate its traditional job of building roads to private companies. But government had never before been in the business of constructing automobile factories or providing jobs to auto workers. It was the expansion of the government's role in the economy that led the court in *Poletown* to declare that the state should aid the auto industry just as it had once aided the construction of railroads.

Nineteenth-century cases allowing the condemnation of property for railroads and private dams had aroused significant controversy at the time.[52] For example, in his famous treatise, *Constitutional Limitations*, Thomas Cooley explained that such condemnations were the exception to a general rule and that the term *"public use* implies a possession, occupation, and enjoyment of the land by the public or public agencies; and there would be no protection whatever to private property, if the right of the government to seize and appropriate it could exist for any other use."[53]

Cooley was serving as chief justice of the Michigan Supreme Court when he wrote those words. Nine years later he again explained the limits on eminent domain in the case of *Ryerson v. Brown*.[54] *Ryerson* was a mill case involving a law that allowed owners of water-powered factories to erect dams that flooded neighboring property. The neighbors sued, arguing that the destruction of their land was for the private use of the mill owners rather than for public use. Cooley pointed out that the legislature, by declaring that "public use" meant whatever use would "in some manner advance the public interest," had endangered all property owners, because "every lawful business does this." If government could condemn property and transfer it to whatever use bureaucrats or the majority of voters considered preferable, the law "would be likely to breed as many grievances as it would cure." True, protecting property rights might sometimes frustrate prospective buyers because landowners could hold out, "but half the value of free institutions consists in the fact that they protect every man in doing what he shall choose, without the liability to be called to account for his reasons or motives, so long as he is doing only that which he has a right to do."[55]

Dissenting in the *Poletown* case over a century later, Justice James Ryan echoed Cooley's words: *every* business reduces unemployment and increases the economic base of the community. In fact, just about anything can plausibly be described as having *some* sort of public benefit. So, if the phrases "public use" and "public benefit" were really synonymous, there would be no limit to the eminent domain power, and the legislature could shift property from owner to owner at will.

But the concerns voiced by Justice Cooley, and then a century later by Justice Ryan, were ignored, both in Michigan and in other states where courts adopted a broad interpretation of "public use" during the second half of the 20th century. In 1958 city officials in Boston demolished the West End, a diverse neighborhood of 20,000 European immigrants and their children. The 50-acre working-class community, fondly remembered by many Bostonians today, was razed in a matter of months to make way for luxury housing.[56] In the decades after World War II, New York's landscape was forever changed by the urban planning of Robert Moses, who demolished thousands of homes in the city to make way for new high-rises, freeways, bridges, and public housing projects.[57] In the early 1980s the California Supreme Court even held that a city could condemn a football team to prevent it from moving to another city.[58]

After *Berman v. Parker* in 1954, the U.S. Supreme Court did not address eminent domain again for 30 years. Then, in 1984 it decided two cases involving the Public Use Clause. In *Ruckelshaus v. Monsanto*,[59] the Court held that the federal government could order a chemical manufacturer to disclose its secret formulas to competing companies, even though the competitors would use the information for their own private gain. The Court rejected "the notion that a use is a public use only if the property taken is put to use for the general public." Rather, if a taking of property "has a conceivable public character," then Congress could take the property. Since it believed that requiring disclosure would "eliminate costly duplication of research," Congress had satisfied the public use requirement.[60]

More famous was *Hawaii Housing v. Midkiff*,[61] involving a state law that allowed residents who owned homes on rented land to request the state to take the land from the landlord and resell it to the tenant at a reduced price. The legislature explained that the law was intended to solve the state's housing shortage, which it claimed was caused by the fact that 47 percent of the state's land was in the hands of about 80 landowners. That, combined with the 49 percent of land owned by the state and federal governments, may have created a housing shortage, but the contention that it had created an "oligopoly" was disingenuous; few economists would regard a market featuring 80 independent sellers as an oligopoly (assuming that term has any precise meaning at all). Nevertheless, the Supreme Court unanimously upheld the law's constitutionality. Relying heavily on *Berman* and New Deal cases, Justice O'Connor wrote that courts had only "extremely narrow" authority to intervene on behalf of landowners.[62] In fact, "where the exercise of the eminent domain power is rationally related to a conceivable public purpose, the Court has never held a compensated taking to be proscribed by the Public Use Clause."[63] This was a very lax standard, indeed. Like *Berman*, both *Monsanto* and *Midkiff* were unanimous decisions.

In the decades after *Berman*, eminent domain expanded to become a routine tool of government planners. Cities and states came to see themselves not as defenders of the rights of citizens but as sculptors of neighborhoods, able to use the property owned by the city's people as the clay that could be molded into an ideal city. In 2003 attorney Dana Berliner of the Institute for Justice published an important study documenting more than 10,000 cases in just the years between 1998 and 2003 in which government officials used eminent domain, or threatened to use it, on behalf of private developers.[64]

Just as President Eisenhower had once warned Americans of the dangers posed by the "military-industrial complex," Berliner's report sounded the alarm about a new threat, the Costco–Ikea–Home Depot–Government complex, through which major corporations and government officials team up to use the power of taking property for mutually profitable projects. The losers in such ventures are the owners of homes and businesses taken to benefit private companies.

The city of Lakewood, Ohio, declared a tidy, middle-class neighborhood "blighted" so that it could make way for a luxury condominium development.[65] The city's standards for determining when a neighborhood was "blighted" included such issues as whether the houses had two-car garages and central air conditioning. After television's *60 Minutes* aired an exposé of this project, voters narrowly defeated the development proposal in a recall election, allowing the homeowners to keep their property.[66] But this outcome is unusual. More often, government is allowed to condemn property to make way for private development. Officials in Wyandotte County, Kansas, condemned land belonging to 150 families to build a NASCAR race track; the state supreme court held that this was constitutional.[67] New York City condemned an entire city block on Times Square to build an office high-rise for the *New York Times*.[68] New York's highest court allowed the condemnation to go forward.[69] In the summer of 2005, Oakland, California, condemned a tire shop and an auto repair business, intending to use the land for a housing development instead.[70] The city also intended to give some of the seized land to Sears so that it could construct a tire shop of its own.[71]

It is ironic that redevelopment projects like these are often put forward by people who claim that neighborhoods need to be revitalized. In fact, such projects often do the opposite: they destroy a community's uniqueness and replace it with the same strip malls with the same shops that can be found in every other city. Urban planners, writes architecture critic Wayne Curtis, don't understand that "the defining unit of a city isn't its buldings. It's the neighborhoods."[72] When redevelopers look at a neighborhood, they see, not a comfortable place to call home, but a blank canvas where they can engage in a government-run "extreme makeover." Redevelopment officials often complain that neighborhoods have a large number of small land parcels, which, they say, prevents developers from "assembling" large lots for shopping centers or similar projects. But, as Curtis explains, a city's vitality and character come from having "a bit of this and a bit of that." Urban redevelopment projects often destroy what makes a city special and replace it with bland, cookie-cutter projects that lack any of the warmth embodied in the word "neighborhood."[73]

Susette Kelo's American Dream

By 2000, the year that the city of New London, Connecticut, decided to condemn the homes of Susette Kelo and her neighbors to construct a hotel, offices, condominiums, and other private commercial facilities, court decisions had given bureaucrats almost unlimited power to redistribute property from one private owner to another.

New London, and particularly its quaint Fort Trumbull neighborhood, had never been particularly prosperous. City officials hoped that the opening of a new Pfizer pharmaceutical plant would be the first step toward economic revitalization in the community. Pfizer, too, wanted to see big changes in the little town. A year earlier representatives from Pfizer and the New London Development Corporation had begun working together on redevelopment plans. The firm Pfizer hired to design its new facility drew up a "vision statement" showing how the city could replace Fort Trumbull with what it called a "high-end residential district" as well as offices, shops, and a marina.[74] Pfizer seems to have told officials that it would locate its new facility there only if the city went forward with plans for redevelopment. A government official anonymously told a local reporter that "they were trying to attract people with Ph.D.s who make $150,000 to $200,000 a year to eastern Connecticut . . . and they were not going to tell them they had to drive to work through a blighted community."[75] Pfizer insists that the redevelopment plans were entirely the city's doing, but whatever the company's level of involvement, it is clear that in 1997 the commissioner of the state's Department of Economic and Community Development wrote to George Milne—a member of the New London Development Corporation and former president of Pfizer's Central Research Division— offering to "defray[] the cost of that development and improv[e] its value through a comprehensive, state-funded waterfront improvement and development project."[76]

Not knowing that secret negotiations were going on, Susette Kelo decided that she had found her dream home. "I searched all over for a house," she recalls, "and finally found this perfect little Victorian cottage with beautiful views of the water." She was working as a paramedic at the time and was "overjoyed that I was able to find a beautiful little place I could afford on my salary. I spent every spare moment fixing it up and creating the kind of home I always dreamed of."[77] She paid $50,000 for the house and then began renovating it. She painted it pink and cleaned up the garden. Over the next few years she met and married a stone mason and fellow antique lover named Tim, and she graduated from nursing school. Tim did the stone work on the house himself, and Susette braided rugs and planted a garden.

Their neighbors, the Derys, lived in two side-by-side houses that the family had owned for more than a century. Wilhelmina Dery was born in one house in 1918 and grew up there. When her sweetheart, Charles, returned from World War II service in the Pacific, they married and opened a grocery store. Despite all the changes in the ensuring decades, the family remained in the homes; the youngest son, Matthew, and his wife and son lived in the second house, which Wilhelmina's mother gave to them as a wedding present.

The day before Thanksgiving 2000, the Kelos, the Derys, and other neighbors received notice that their homes were going to be condemned. "We did not have a very pleasant holiday," recalls Susette Kelo, "and each Thanksgiving since has been bittersweet for all of us."[78] Interestingly, the Italian Dramatic Club, a social organization located next door to one of the condemned houses, was also originally slated for demolition, but in 2000 it was mysteriously informed that it would be allowed to remain. That may have had something to do with the fact that the club was frequented by many prominent Connecticut politicians, including then-governor John Rowland.

The Kelos and six other families sued, arguing that the condemnation of their property violated the "public use" requirement of both the Connecticut and the U.S. Constitutions. In a four-to-three decision, the Connecticut Supreme Court upheld the condemnation. The majority indignantly rejected the notion that the Public Use Clauses require anything more than a general benefit to the public. The Connecticut Constitution "requires only that the 'benefit' of the taking be available to the general public," the court held. The "massive projected growths in employment and tax and other revenues" that city planners expected the development to bring were enough to sustain the condemnation. The court was so eager to expand legislative authority that it even declared that Michigan's *Poletown* decision had been *too protective* of property owners!

But while the U.S. Supreme Court was considering whether to review the *Kelo* case, the Michigan Supreme Court made a startling announcement: it overruled the *Poletown* decision,[79] declaring that it had given government too much leeway to take private property. By equating "public use" with "public benefit," and by eliminating the Due Process Clause's prohibition on redistributions of property to private parties, court decisions such as *Poletown* had opened the floodgates to seizures of property by whatever private interest group was most effective in exploiting government power. What Thomas Hobbes once said of the chaos in a world without law was coming true in America: "[T]here could be no [property], no dominion, no *mine* and *thine* distinct, but only that to be every man's that he can get: and for so long as he can keep it."[80]

Recognizing the dangerous fallout of allowing government to take property for any asserted "public benefit," the Michigan Supreme Court concluded:

> Every business, every productive unit in society, does ... contribute in some way to the commonwealth. To justify the exercise of eminent domain solely on the basis of the fact that the use of that property by a private entity seeking its own profit might contribute to the economy's health is to render impotent our constitutional limitations on the government's power of eminent domain. *Poletown*'s "economic benefit" rationale would validate practically any exercise of the power of eminent domain on behalf of a private entity. After

> all, if one's ownership of private property is forever subject
> to the government's determination that another private party
> would put one's land to better use, then the ownership of
> real property is perpetually threatened by the expansion
> plans of any large discount retailer, "megastore," or the like.[81]

Still, the court tried to strike a balance between the rights of property owners and what it saw as the necessity for government to eradicate slum property. It described three categories of cases in which eminent domain would be permitted, even if government transferred property to the use of a private party: cases involving highways, railroads, and the like; cases in which the property would be transferred to a government-run or government-regulated entity such as a public utility; and cases in which "the underlying purpose for resorting to condemnation, rather than the subsequent use of condemned land," serves the public generally, which seemed to mean cases involving dilapidated or dangerous property.[82]

The end of the *Poletown* case encouraged defenders of property rights to hope that the U.S. Supreme Court would also see fit to rein in the power of eminent domain. Unfortunately, that hope would be dashed. The Court took the *Kelo* case, but in a five-to-four decision it agreed with the Connecticut Supreme Court: legislatures and city officials have virtually unlimited discretion to take away citizens' homes and businesses and use the property for private development projects.

Justice John Paul Stevens explained that "public use" and "public benefit" were synonymous, and since "promoting economic development is a traditional and long accepted function of government," the city could condemn the homes of the Kelo and Dery families to transfer the property to private developers. Any more restrictive interpretation of the eminent domain power would be "difficult to administer"[83] and might intrude on the legislature's ability to serve the needs of the business community. Stevens cited the railroad and dam cases to show that the Court had never taken the term "public use" literally but had always "defined that concept broadly, reflecting our longstanding policy of deference to legislative judgments."[84]

As with the *Poletown* case, the kernel of Stevens's decision lies in his assertion that promoting economic development is a proper governmental function. Stevens gave no justification for that claim; he simply took it for granted. After all, the Court's decisions since

Nebbia v. New York had given the government almost boundless power to manage the economy. The limits on eminent domain have always paralleled society's understanding of the proper role of government. When government was not considered the primary engine of economic progress, courts held that eminent domain could be used only for genuinely public projects such as roads and post offices, but as government's role in the economy expanded, courts came to blur the line between public and private enterprises. Fostering economic growth—once seen as an affair for private businesses— now became a governmental function and thus a proper use of eminent domain.

The concept of due process of law is also inextricably tied to the nation's understanding of government's proper function. When lawyers debate whether the Due Process Clause has been violated in a particular case, they use such formulas as "rationally related to a legitimate government interest" or "narrowly tailored to a legitimate government interest." When a law doesn't appropriately serve a "legitimate interest," the Due Process Clause has been violated. Yet in 1987 the Supreme Court admitted that it had "not elaborated on the standards for determining what constitutes a 'legitimate state interest.'"[85] That is a remarkable statement indeed! The nation's highest court was admitting that it did not know what the proper purposes of government are. Without such an understanding, however, the Court is, as Roger Pilon has put it, "without a compass."[86] As a result, the Court could only step back and allow the legislature to expand its power over matters America's Founders would have considered off limits, including "promoting economic development" by taking property from some and giving it to others. It came as a shock to some that the four "liberals" on the *Kelo* Court—Stevens, Souter, Breyer, and Ginsburg—upheld the constitutionality of such a massive corporate welfare program. But it shouldn't have surprised anyone: the decision was an obvious step in a gradual progression away from security in private property and toward a world in which government can treat people's homes and businesses as the raw materials with which to sculpt the bureaucrats' notion of an ideal city.

By contrasting two passages from decisions of the Court separated by almost a century and a half, one can see clearly the drift away from the principles of the American founding. In 1829 the Supreme

Court said: "We know of no case, in which a legislative act to transfer the property of A. to B. without his consent, has ever been held a constitutional exercise of legislative power in any state in the union. On the contrary, it has been constantly resisted as inconsistent with just principles, by every judicial tribunal in which it has been attempted to be enforced."[87] But in 1978 the Court held that the Fifth Amendment does not require compensation when government takes a person's property so as to "adjust[] the benefits and burdens of economic life."[88] The distance between those two conceptions of government's proper role indicates the reversal that took place in constitutional law during the 20th century. That reversal was responsible for the *Kelo* decision, which explicitly allows government to transfer the property of A to B without A's consent so that bureaucrats can adjust the benefits and burdens of economic life as they see fit.

Four justices dissented in *Kelo*, and their dissents are interesting for two reasons. First, the lead dissent was written by Justice Sandra Day O'Connor, who had written the unanimous *Midkiff* decision 20 years earlier. In that case she had declared that government may redistribute property between private owners in almost any circumstance. But in *Kelo* she tried to spin that decision differently. *Midkiff* and *Berman*, she wrote, involved property that was being used in ways that "inflicted affirmative harm on society" so that "a public purpose was realized when the harmful use was eliminated." The Kelos and the Derys, by contrast, were not harming society in any way with their "well-maintained homes."[89] Therefore, *Berman* and *Midkiff* did not really apply. And in any case, to allow condemnation of property simply because the legislature thinks it could produce more revenue in the hands of another owner would mean that "nothing is to prevent the State from replacing any Motel 6 with a Ritz-Carlton, any home with a shopping mall, or any farm with a factory."[90]

O'Connor was right to be outraged, but her attempt to distinguish *Kelo* from earlier cases was weak, and Justice Stevens pounced on it. The older cases had *not* involved property that "inflicted affirmative harm on society": Max Morris's department store, which gave rise to the *Berman* case, was not blighted or dangerous in any way, and certainly the trade secrets that the government "took" in the *Monsanto* case weren't.[91] Stevens, in short, called O'Connor's bluff:

102

if her decision in *Midkiff* meant what it said—that government can take property from some and give it to others whenever doing so serves the legislature's view of the public welfare—there is no reason it could not do the same thing in the *Kelo* case. O'Connor tried to dismiss the important elements of her *Midkiff* decision by describing it as "errant language," but the decision had been unanimous, and there was no denying that the Court had meant what it said.[92]

Unlike Justice O'Connor's dissenting opinion, Justice Clarence Thomas's dissent reflected a sincere willingness to reexamine the underlying principles of *Berman* and *Midkiff*. Noting the disastrous effect that eminent domain tends to have on minority property owners, he criticized the Court for abandoning its traditional concern for groups that lack political power. "Extending the concept of public purpose to encompass any economically beneficial goal guarantees that these losses will fall disproportionately on poor communities," he wrote.

> Those communities are not only systematically less likely to put their lands to the highest and best social use, but are also the least politically powerful. If ever there were justification for intrusive judicial review of constitutional provisions that protect "discrete and insular minorities," surely that principle would apply with great force to the powerless groups and individuals the Public Use Clause protects.[93]

But most important, the decisions equating "public use" with "public benefit" had originated with the Court's abandonment of economic liberty and private property rights during the New Deal era. Decisions following *Nebbia*, Thomas noted, created a bizarre double standard under which property rights receive virtually no protection from the courts while other, preferred, rights receive much greater solicitude. "We would not defer to a legislature's determination of the various circumstances that establish, for example, when a search of a home would be reasonable, or when a convicted double-murderer may be shackled during a sentencing proceeding," and yet the Court does defer to a legislature's determination of what satisfies the Public Use Clause.[94] That dichotomy makes no sense.

> The Court has elsewhere recognized "the overriding respect for the sanctity of the home that has been embedded in our traditions since the origins of the Republic," when the issue

103

> is only whether the government may search a home. Yet today the Court tells us that we are not to "second-guess the City's considered judgments," when the issue is, instead, whether the government may take the infinitely more intrusive step of tearing down petitioners' homes. Something has gone seriously awry with this Court's interpretation of the Constitution. Though citizens are safe from the government in their homes, the homes themselves are not.[95]

As for Stevens's theory that the taking of the Kelos' and Derys' homes for private development was justified by the old railroad and dam cases, Justice Thomas explained that Stevens was overlooking the way those cases had subjected the railroads and dams to heavy government regulation, which made them into public utilities.[96] No such regulations were involved here; the property would not be used for a semipublic transportation system. Instead, the homeowners were being evicted to make way for property owners that the government considered more appealing.

The second thing that makes the dissents of Justices O'Connor and Thomas special is that they represent the first time since at least the 1930s that any justice of the Supreme Court has held that the eminent domain power is limited in any way.[97] While defenders of property rights have much to complain about in the *Kelo* decision, those dissents show that some progress has been made: four of the justices—including the author of *Midkiff*—have come to realize that there must be some limits if property owners are to be safe from uncontrollable and arbitrary interference by legislatures. That is indeed reason for optimism. For more than 70 years, Supreme Court justices have been willing, almost without exception, to abide some of the most extreme violations of individual rights in the name of "democratic decisionmaking." That some are having second thoughts is certainly gratifying.

Nevertheless, as the law stands today, property owners are almost entirely at the mercy of the state, and all property is owned subject to virtually unpredictable revocation by state authorities. Although some state constitutions—such as Michigan's—do protect property owners against the abuse of eminent domain, the Supreme Court has washed its hands of the issue as far as the federal Constitution is concerned.

State law can protect property owners even when federal law does not, but in many states, those protections are illusory. Under California law, for example, property cannot be condemned for economic redevelopment until after the government has declared it "blighted." This led many people to believe that Californians had nothing to worry about from the *Kelo* decision because that case was only about property that had not been declared blighted. Yet California's legal definition of "blight" is so lax that almost any property in the state can be targeted for condemnation. Among the legal criteria for declaring property blighted in California are "[f]actors that . . . substantially hinder the economically viable use . . . of buildings . . . [including] substandard design, inadequate size given present standards and market conditions, [or] lack of parking," "adjacent or nearby uses that are incompatible with each other and which prevent the economic development of . . . the project area," and "the existence of subdivided lots of irregular form and shape and inadequate size for proper usefulness and development that are in multiple ownership."[98] Under such standards a local government can declare virtually any property blighted.

Worse, once a city declares a neighborhood blighted, that designation never expires. It can remain on the books for decades, like a bomb waiting to go off, until a property owner discovers that his property is being condemned. And a property owner has no serious opportunity to challenge a blight designation in court. Once a city council declares property blighted, a court will defer to that decision almost without exception. Finally, contrary to the claims of many redevelopment officials, not only blighted property can be condemned. Any property *in a blighted area* can be condemned, even if the property itself is not blighted—much like the unblighted department store that was condemned in the *Berman* case. In 2001 the Rados Brothers of Chula Vista, California, lost a three-acre tract when the government decided to give it to the B. F. Goodrich tire company pursuant to a blight designation that was 30 years old. In fact, the property was not blighted, but a state court allowed it to be taken anyway because it was near property that had been declared blighted.[99] "Collateral damage," so to speak.

After the *Kelo* case was decided, several states started to reform their eminent domain laws to better protect citizens.[100] But so far few states have established any meaningful reforms. Alabama, for

105

example, quickly passed a law that was hailed by many pundits as the first serious reaction against *Kelo*, but in reality it accomplishes little. It only imposes a rule, similar to California's, that officials must declare land "blighted" before condemning it.[101] But it does nothing to fix Alabama's vague definition of "blight," which includes buildings that suffer from "obsolescence," "faulty arrangement or design," "lack of ventilation," "excessive land coverage," or "other factors."[102] More brazen was the reform measure passed in Texas, which was amended at the last minute to allow the Dallas Cowboys to condemn property in Arlington and build a sports stadium.[103] The California legislature killed three different proposals for prohibiting or even just temporarily halting the use of eminent domain to benefit private companies,[104] while Delaware passed a law that merely requires bureaucrats to tell property owners *why* they're taking the property six months before they do so.[105]

In the spring of 2006, the Virginia legislature refused to enact limits on eminent domain, and although the New Mexico legislature passed a strong reform bill, it was vetoed by Governor Bill Richardson. Worst of all, Ohio enacted a law that simply imposes a one-year moratorium on condemnations for economic development, while a bureaucratic committee of 25 members writes a report on the use of eminent domain in the state. This committee is carefully chosen to include many defenders of the redevelopment industry, and once the report is finished the legislature is not required to act on its recommendations at all; it can simply ignore the report and go back to condemning property. Moreover, the moratorium does not apply at all to redevelopment projects already under way in cities such as Cincinnati or Cleveland, which led one reporter to comment that the law would have "minimal impact."[106] In fact, as of this writing, the only state to enact a meaningful limit on eminent domain is South Dakota—a state that appears never to have abused the power anyway.[107]

Still, some states have taken their duty to protect property owners seriously. Not only Michigan, but Illinois, Arizona, Washington, and several other states have constitutional provisions specifically prohibiting the condemnation of private property for private use. Those state constitutions are important because, after *Kelo*, they and the state courts that enforce them are the only protection property owners have.

Procedural Roadblocks

Property owners also face serious procedural obstacles when they try to protect their rights. Special rules apply to them that don't apply to people trying to protect any other kinds of rights. Those rules limit their opportunity for judicial review and cause court delays that can stretch on for years, even decades, making litigation prohibitively expensive. As a result, many property owners do not even file suit.

Palazzolo v. Rhode Island[108] suggests some of the obstacles property owners typically face. In the 1960s Anthony Palazzolo bought 18 acres in Rhode Island, intending to construct homes he could sell to provide for his retirement. He purchased the property at first in the name of a corporation of which he was the sole shareholder. While the property was technically owned by his corporation, the state passed a law forbidding construction on anything that was designated as a "wetland." Realizing that such a law would require the state to pay Palazzolo for the value of his land, bureaucrats quickly revised their rules, claiming that they would allow him to build a single house on the property. That reduced the value of the property from $3.1 million to about $200,000.[109] Then in 1978, after the law was in place, Palazzolo dissolved his corporation, which meant that he came to own the property in his own name, and he began the process of seeking government permission to build on the land. When permission was denied, he filed a lawsuit, arguing that the state had deprived him of all of the economic value of his property.

The Rhode Island Supreme Court rejected his claim. When the property came to him in his own name in 1978, it explained, Palazzolo was aware that the state had prohibited development. Anybody who acquires property after the enactment of a land-use regulation, the court held, "take[s] the land subject to preexisting limitations and without the compensation then owed to the original affected owner."[110] Under this "notice rule," subsequent property owners— in this case, Mr. Palazzolo himself—would be barred from challenging the constitutionality of any law enacted before they obtained their property—no matter how outrageous that law might be.

Fortunately, the U.S. Supreme Court overruled that decision. The notice rule would, the Court declared, "put an expiration date on the Takings Clause."[111] Palazzolo should have the right to challenge the constitutionality of the law even though it had been on the books for years. Yet while the decision seemed to promise greater protection for landowners, Justice O'Connor wrote a separate opinion that ended up sabotaging that hope. In some cases, she argued, the timing of the law's enactment would be considered among the other factors in the subjective *Penn Central* test. In other words, a court could still deny compensation because it could still rule that it was unreasonable for Palazzolo to expect that he could use his property. Thanks to O'Connor's separate decision, the notice rule still continues to afflict property owners.[112]

An even more severe obstacle is what lawyers refer to as the "*Williamson County* trap." According to a case called *Williamson County*,[113] property owners who want just compensation for regulatory takings must first file a lawsuit in state court, not federal court. But state courts are almost always unwilling to compensate property owners, even in truly egregious cases. Worse, due to a concept that lawyers call "preclusion," once a person loses in state court, federal courts are required to follow the decisions of the state courts and are not allowed to even consider different legal theories that the property owner might want to argue. Thus, unlike any other kind of plaintiff, property owners are barred from filing lawsuits in federal court at the outset; they are required to go to state court, where they will very likely lose, and their only recourse then is to appeal to the U.S. Supreme Court, which hears only about 80 cases per year.

In the 2005 case involving the San Remo Hotel,[114] the Supreme Court even barred property owners from asking state courts to hold off ruling on their federal law claims as a way of preserving those claims for a hearing before a federal judge. As Chief Justice Rehnquist noted, the *Williamson County* trap "all but guarantees that claimants will be unable to utilize the federal courts to enforce the Fifth Amendment's just compensation guarantee."[115] This is especially unfortunate, since the Fourteenth Amendment was designed precisely to provide a separate federal route for people who cannot get justice in state courts. The trap applies *only* to property owners; in a case involving any other kind of constitutional right—from freedom of speech to the right to vote—a person bringing a lawsuit would have a choice of whether to go to state or federal court.

There are several other rules that bar property owners from getting their day in court. For instance, property owners must wait for their claim to "ripen" before they can file suit—meaning that government must make some final decision about the use of their property. But because land-use bureaucrats are aware of this rule, they tend to take as long as possible before issuing a final decision. They can delay for years, calling for more hearings, more research, more permit applications, or more negotiations, dragging out the process until owners give up or go broke.[116]

Civil Asset Forfeiture

Another growing danger to property rights arises from a little-known area of the law called civil asset forfeiture.[117] Federal and state laws provide for the seizure of property—real estate, money, cars, boats, any kind of property—if it can be said to have "facilitated" a crime.

Based on a medieval superstition that property can itself be "guilty" of a crime, asset forfeiture cases are brought, not against a human defendant, but against the property itself.[118] This means that asset forfeiture laws need not meet the same standards as normal criminal laws. In a criminal trial, the burden of proof is on the state to prove that the defendant committed the crime. But in asset forfeiture cases, the burden of proof is generally on the property owner to prove that the property is "innocent." In those states that do put the burden of proof on the government in forfeiture cases, the government is not required to meet the usual criminal level of proof known as "beyond a reasonable doubt"; instead, it need only meet the much lower standard of "preponderance of the evidence."[119] Nor do other constitutional protections apply the way they do for human defendants: there is no right to an attorney, and the property's owner does not have to be convicted before the property can be seized. Some 80 percent of civil asset forfeitures are undertaken without any criminal prosecution at all,[120] and property can be taken even if the owner was not aware that a crime was being committed with it. Nor does civil asset forfeiture qualify as a "taking" of property for public use under the Fifth Amendment; because the property is seized under the government's *police power*, rather than under the power of eminent domain, the government is not required to compensate the owner.

To make matters worse, civil asset forfeiture laws often allow law enforcement agencies to keep the property they seize, creating an enormous incentive for police departments to abuse their power. In 1998 the federal government seized more than $696 million in forfeitures.[121] In one case, officers seized more than half a million dollars from a restaurant, arguing that normal people don't have that much cash lying around.[122] A federal appeals court later ordered the police to return the money, noting that the police had "provided absolutely no preliminary showing of probable cause." The judges went on to criticize police and prosecutors for their "increasing and virtually unchecked use of the civil forfeiture statutes and the disregard for the due process that is buried in those statutes."[123]

Unfortunately, courts are not always so willing to protect innocent property owners from forfeiture laws. In 1997 Tina Bennis's husband John picked up a prostitute on the way home from working the night shift. After the Detroit police caught him in the act in his car, they filed suit to seize the car as a "nuisance" under Michigan law, even though Tina co-owned the car and had certainly not consented to her husband's action. A state court ruled in her favor, finding that "the prosecutor was required to prove that [Mrs. Bennis] knew that their vehicle was being used" for an illegal purpose.[124] But the Michigan Supreme Court overruled that decision, holding that in forfeiture cases the owner's innocence doesn't matter.[125] The U.S. Supreme Court agreed. "She did not know that her car would be used in an illegal activity that would subject it to forfeiture,"[126] wrote Chief Justice Rehnquist, but that made no difference, because "'the thing is here primarily considered as the offender.'"[127]

Abuses of civil asset forfeiture abound. In 1991 Houston florist Willie Jones aroused suspicion at the Nashville Airport when he bought a plane ticket with cash. When Drug Enforcement Administration officers found that he was traveling with $9,000 in cash, they seized the money.[128] Jones explained that he was purchasing shrubbery for his landscaping business and sellers prefer to deal in cash. Although the government never convicted him of a drug-related crime, or even charged him, it kept the money for more than two years until a federal court ordered the money returned. The forfeiture laws, the court noted, "provide substantial opportunity for abuse and potentiality for corruption." Drug enforcement officers "encourage airline employees as well as hotel and motel employees to report 'suspicious' travelers and reward them with a percentage of the forfeited proceeds." Officers were not even required to record or report the amount of seized money they took and spent. Such laws, the court concluded, are "an unsavory and embarrassing scar on the administration of justice."[129]

In 1989 DEA officers in California seized a private jet when they found $2.7 million in cash in the luggage of a passenger who had flown in from Arkansas. Although the owner and pilot of the jet, Bill Munnerlyn, had not known about the money, and charges against him were eventually dropped, the agency kept the jet. Munnerlyn had to sell several other planes to pay his lawyer's fee of $80,000, but the agency refused to return the jet until he paid $66,000. When he finally got the plane back for $7,000, he discovered that agents had done $50,000 worth of damage to it while searching for evidence—damage for which the agency was not required to pay. The costs drove Munnerlyn out of the piloting business.[130]

On October 2, 1992, 30 drug agents from various agencies broke down the door of a Malibu, California, ranch house owned by 62-year-old Donald Scott. Scott, who was sleeping upstairs, grabbed a pistol and ran downstairs to defend his terrified wife from the masked intruders. They shot him dead in front of her. The search for marijuana plants on Scott's 200 acres turned up nothing. A later investigation found that the warrant had been issued on the basis of the unverified say-so of a single informant and that the officers who sought the warrant lied about the evidence. The Ventura County district attorney concluded "that the Los Angeles County Sheriff's Department was motivated, at least in part, by a desire to seize and forfeit the ranch for the government."[131]

In response to such abuses, Congress passed and President Clinton signed into law the Civil Asset Forfeiture Reform Act in 2000.[132] The act, which applies only to federal actions, shifted the burden of proof to the government and provided some protection for impoverished innocent people who might lose their homes to forfeiture. But it did not stop seized money from going to law enforcement agencies, which creates the greatest incentive for official wrongdoing.[133] And of course the act had no effect on state laws.

Realizing their need for greater protection, citizens of Utah passed a statewide initiative in 2000 that restricted the state's use of forfeiture.[134] The law enforcement community waged an expensive campaign against it, but the reform passed by a landslide vote of 69 percent, so the police challenged the law in court. When a federal

111

judge upheld it as constitutional,[135] the law enforcement community tried to get it repealed. That attempt failed, too, so the district attorneys of three counties simply refused to follow the law. A state auditor found that those counties were "disregarding" the law by holding on to hundreds of thousands of dollars of seized property that, under the reform measure, ought to have been transferred to the state's education fund.[136] Yet the state's attorney general did nothing. Finally, a group of citizens, represented by the Institute for Justice, notified officials that they would soon sue them for their lawlessness.[137] At that point, the district attorneys said they would give up the money, but in 2004 the state legislature caved in to this official civil disobedience and passed a bill changing key provisions of the reform measure, once again allowing the law enforcement community to keep the money it seizes.[138]

The Attack on Private Property

In virtually every area of the law, from asset forfeiture laws to environmental regulations to the rules governing building permits and how to file lawsuits, private property is treated, in Chief Justice Rehnquist's phrase, like "a poor relation,"[139] a second-class member of the Bill of Rights. In many cases, violations of property rights result from well-intended attempts to improve society. But whether their goals are laudable or not, officials must learn to respect the private property rights of people who do not share their vision, or who do not want to bear the whole cost of providing a benefit to the public. If the history of government has taught us anything, it is that good intentions aren't enough; they are often the source of the worst abuses.

Take, for example, economic development projects that involve eminent domain. Some of those projects have probably succeeded in improving local economies. But they have done so at tremendous costs: the demolition of family homes, the violation of privacy and personal freedoms, the destruction of sentimental value, and a growing cynicism about democratic institutions. Worse, one violation of private property rights creates a precedent for another, and that for another, until the line dividing good intentions from bad is unclear. That is nowhere more obvious than in redevelopment cases. Because of the problem of rent seeking, redevelopment projects routinely evict lower-class and minority property owners, transferring the property to powerful, wealthy companies. It is not always easy to distinguish between projects that really are intended to "clean up the neighborhood" and those that are meant to push out "undesirable" minorities. In one incident, an attorney for Costco, lobbying the planning commission of Lenexa, Kansas, told officials that they ought to condemn a community to make way for a Costco store because it was "not much of a neighborhood, anyway."[140] One is reminded of the famous line from Daniel Webster's argument before the Supreme Court in *Dartmouth College v. Woodward*: "It is, Sir, as I have said, a small college. And yet there are those who love it!"[141]

In other cases, government's purposes are more sinister. The California Coastal Commission was created by a 1972 law drafted in large part by Peter Douglas, an outspoken opponent of private property rights.[142] Douglas was quickly chosen executive director of the commission, where he has remained for three decades. Environmentalism, Douglas believes, is "about struggle against dehumanizing, amoral corporate capitalism and imperialism at all levels around the planet, and environmental destruction resulting from greed and materialism."[143]

Like a character from Michael Crichton's *State of Fear*, Douglas proudly calls himself a "social engineer" and a "radical."[144] He has advocated amending the federal Constitution to guarantee a right to welfare.[145] Like many opponents of property rights, Douglas believes that property is not a natural part of the human personality but is instead created by government, which "give[s] certain public interests over to private possession."[146] Government creates private property, he argues, because "exploitive extractive corporate industries," acting out of "corporate greed," have fooled the "unwary populace."[147] The human desire for private property is the result of the overpowering "materialism and greed of society" by which "people are conditioned from birth to crave stuff, especially stuff we don't need."[148] But because "the corporate takeover of vital sectors of our world" leads to environmental destruction, "environmental groups must be radical and address the root causes. . . . They must not buy into the politics of accommodation. . . ."[149] In particular, Douglas argues, environmentalists must not just urge people to keep the environment clean but must also use the law to "chang[e] individual and collective behavior of people."[150]

Douglas is unafraid to admit his willingness to use force, instead of persuasion, against people who want to use the land they own.

"Strong government regulation, in perpetuity, is absolutely essential," he argues.[151] He believes that the deliberation, negotiation, mutual agreement, and respect for private property that most people consider essential to democratic decisionmaking would simply get in the way. "Conciliation has value," he writes, but "[p]ragmatism, consensus decision-making and the politics of accommodation must not trump . . . progressive positions on important environmental protection issues."[152]

Douglas admits that the laws he advocates will deprive many people of the value of their land. But he resists paying just compensation because "there simply is not enough money to pay the bill," and "there will never be enough money."[153] Therefore, ways must be found to force private landowners, rather than the public, to bear the costs. As for people or organizations that believe in defending private property, Douglas believes that they are merely pawns of evil corporations; they don't represent "real" people.

The California Coastal Commission has supreme authority over development along the state's shoreline and, as the executive director, Douglas has exploited this power to strangle construction on the California coast. His reign has been a case study in the abuse of government authority: imposing endless delays on development, carefully avoiding final decisions that might give property owners an opportunity to sue, requiring developers to negotiate with hand-picked activists who he knows will bar development, and imposing perverse interpretations of the law to stretch the commission's authority.

For example, the commission recently announced that it would prohibit any construction that might be seen from boats at sea, reasoning that its legal authority to "protect views *to and along* the ocean and scenic coastal areas" includes the power to protect views *from* the ocean as well. When a county court upheld the commission's authority,[154] Douglas praised the ruling because "undeveloped shoreline is a very unique and valuable resource."[155] Indeed it is, but Douglas does not want to pay for it. Instead, his commission has imposed that cost on property owners who have invested their money in hopes of building their dream homes. Yet Douglas laughs at such considerations: "We have wealthy people who can afford to buy remote rural ranches—which they have no intention of working as ranches—but they want to build a starter castle there."

Of course, if people want to buy "castles," they have that right. As Sir Edward Coke explained four centuries ago, "[T]he house of every one is to him as his castle and fortress."[156] But not under Peter Douglas's rule. When George and Sharlee McNamee installed a canopy, barbeque, shower, and picnic tables in their sandy Corona Del Mar back yard, they received an ultimatum from the commission: remove them or face $6,000 per day in fines. The commission's reason for telling the McNamees what they could put in their back yard was that installing their barbeque area discouraged the public from using nearby beaches by creating a "perception of privatization."[157] Their challenge to the commission is still pending in court.

The commission's control over people seeking to construct new homes is even more extreme, and the commission is capable of trapping them in enormous spider webs of red tape. Kenneth Healing found that out when he bought land in the Santa Monica mountains in 1977. He planned to build a modest three-bedroom home on the land. But when he applied to the commission for permission to build, the bureaucrats refused to make any decision. The county had not yet devised a legal plan for development in the area, and the commission believed that allowing Healing to build would make it impossible to get such a plan approved by the right authorities. So the commission delayed its decision for *12 years*. Finally, the commission denied Healing's request on the grounds that it could not determine what effect his house might have on the environment. The county had not yet created an environmental review board to evaluate building permit requests, they explained. Of course, the county promised to create such a board someday, if it ever got around to it. In the meantime, the commission claimed that Healing could not sue because it had not really made a decision one way or the other on his permit application, so his case was not "ripe." Healing was stuck in legal no man's land, waiting for the county to create a bureaucracy to review his request to build on his own property.

Finally, in 1990 Healing sued anyway, and after four years of litigation—17 years after he bought his land—the California Court of Appeal ruled in his favor. "The County has been trying since 1982 to obtain certification of its [land use plan]," the court noted.

> Meanwhile, along comes poor Healing who . . . applies to
> the Coastal Commission for a permit to build his house, only

> to be told by the Commission that, because the Commission
> has not approved the County's [plan], the Commission can't
> say one way or the other . . . and, as far as the Commission
> is concerned, its failure to act one way or the other means
> there has been no denial of a permit which, in turn, means
> Healing's complaints are not "ripe" for judicial review—and
> may never be so.[158]

The commission's decades-long delay in processing Healing's application was "beyond both the ridiculous and the sublime. . . . To state the Coastal Commission's position is to demonstrate its absurdity."[159] But although he finally won his case, and a $350,000 judgment against the government, Healing never got his dream house. He ended up selling the land to the Santa Monica Coastal Conservancy. As my colleague at the Pacific Legal Foundation, J. David Breemer, writes: Healing's case "is hardly an anomaly. In case after case, the Commission has found a way to prevent the reasonable use of established private property interests . . . [and] to create precedents that expand its powers to control the private use of coastal land."[160]

America's Founding Fathers understood the importance of private property rights to individuals and to society: property allows people to pursue happiness, to get along with those who differ from them, and to rest secure in the knowledge that the fruits of their hard work will not be taken away. Unfortunately, modern political leaders have come to ignore the lessons the Founders taught. From the halls of Congress to city hall, government at every level infringes on private property rights with regulations that take away the value of land or seize homes and businesses outright to transfer them to people bureaucrats believe are better suited to use them—or even to the bureaucrats themselves. Correcting such abuses and preventing future injustices are essential for securing our nation's prosperity and protecting the homes and dreams of Americans.

5. What Can Be Done?

Despite politicians' rhetoric of an "ownership society," and despite the American Constitution's guarantees of security for private property rights, government at the federal, state, and local level interferes in almost every aspect of ownership, overriding people's decisions to buy, build, rent, or even own their land at all. How, then, can the crisis of ownership be resolved? What follows are a few suggestions for increasing protections for the owners of private property.

Eminent Domain

The Supreme Court's decision in *Kelo v. New London* means that citizens cannot look to the federal Constitution for protection. Instead, they must receive protections from their state constitutions. The death of Chief Justice Rehnquist and the retirement of Justice O'Connor will not undermine the *Kelo* decision because both were on the dissenting side.

One federal reform recently approved by the House[1] would restrict the use of federal funding for economic development projects involving eminent domain. If enacted, that proposal would be an enormous benefit for property owners because many development projects are funded by federal dollars. Even the *Poletown* condemnation was made possible by $200 million in grants from Washington.[2]

Since state laws and constitutions can provide greater protections for citizens than federal law does, amending state constitutions to make clear that "public use" really means "public use," and not private use, may be necessary in states where courts have allowed the transfer of property under the "economic benefit" rationale. Although *Kelo* set off a national outcry over government's abuse of property rights, only one state, South Dakota, has so far adopted an effective limit on its eminent domain authority. Some state courts, including those of Michigan[3] and Illinois,[4] have recently held that

117

their state constitutions already prohibit economic development condemnations. But in other states constitutional amendment is the only way to truly protect people from eminent domain abuse.

There are three ways of doing that. The first is to adopt language from the constitution of a state that already forbids the use of eminent domain for private parties. The constitutions of Washington and Arizona, for example, already declare that "[p]rivate property shall not be taken for private use" and that whenever the legislature claims that it is taking property for a public use, "the question whether the contemplated use be really public shall be a judicial question, and determined as such, without regard to any legislative assertion that the use is public."[5] Both states have found that the economic benefits of transferring property from one person to another are not enough to satisfy the public use requirement.[6] However, the Washington Supreme Court recently weakened its protections in a case holding that the government may condemn a wide area of land around a train station and use it for private shops.[7] By importing identical provisions into their constitutions, other states could benefit from that more explicit language. But if Arizona and Washington courts continue to weaken those provisions, this technique will probably not be helpful.

A second alternative is to devise new language entirely. This is difficult because the difference between a public use and a private use is not very clear in the modern regulatory state. Forbidding government from *giving* or *selling* any property to a private party would be easy to evade: government could simply lease out the land it takes for $1. But a prohibition on leasing property taken through eminent domain might go too far: it would bar shoe-shine stands in government office buildings or bookshops in airports. Likewise, requiring property taken through eminent domain to be used exclusively by government agencies would, if applied literally, mean that only government-owned cars could use a state's highways! Another solution would be simply to list everything for which eminent domain may be used, but that would be tedious and would invite amendments that would expand the power over time.

A more effective solution was attempted in a recent California bill that would have amended the state constitution to forbid government from giving or leasing seized property to any private party except those regulated by the state's public utilities commission (and also specifically allowing for shops in government-owned buildings).[8] But that bill was killed by the powerful opposition of redevelopment agencies.[9] Another option would be to define "public use" by copying the factors from the recent Michigan Supreme Court decision overturning *Poletown*. The court there allowed the government to take property and transfer it to private entities to build highways, railroads, and other instrumentalities of commerce, or to construct public utilities, or to eliminate property that is dangerous to the general public.[10] Although those factors would still allow too many condemnations to go forward, such an approach would be a significant improvement over the present rules of many states. The Michigan Legislature, in fact, has drafted a constitutional amendment and submitted it for voter approval, which would put the burden of proof on the government to prove that a proposed condemnation is for public use, and which prohibits the taking of property "for transfer to a private entity for the purpose of economic development or the enhancement of tax revenues." It also would require the state to pay homeowners 125 percent of the value of residences that it takes.[11]

Lawyers at the Institute for Justice and other organizations have drafted model constitutional amendments to prevent eminent domain abuse. The Institute's proposal reads:

> With just compensation paid, private property may be taken only when necessary for the possession, occupation, or enjoyment of land by the public at large, or by public agencies. Except for privately owned common carriers, private property shall not be taken for use by private commercial enterprise, for economic development, or for any other private use, except with the consent of the owner. Property shall not be taken from one owner and transferred to another, on the grounds that the public will benefit from a more profitable private use. Whenever an attempt is made to take private property for a use alleged to be public, the question whether the contemplated use be really public shall be a judicial question, and determined as such without regard to any legislative assertion that the use is public.[12]

Likewise, the Reason Foundation has drafted several proposals, including the following:

> Notwithstanding any other provision of law, neither this State nor any political subdivisions thereof nor any other condemnor shall use eminent domain to take private property without the consent of the owner to be used for economic development. Whenever property is condemned and will be used by a private party, the condemnor must establish by clear and convincing evidence that the condemnation of the property is necessary.[13]

Amendments like these would provide an enormous benefit to home and business owners in states where eminent domain is now out of control.

Defining "Blight"

Many if not most of the abusive eminent domain cases in recent years have been undertaken as part of government efforts to eliminate "blight." Whether government should be involved in such undertakings in the first place is highly questionable. A good case can be made that government efforts to boost development are ultimately harmful to the economy, since the benefits it gives to businesses must be taken from other people in the first place. For example, it seems likely that Detroit ended up destroying as many jobs as it "created" in the *Poletown* case when it demolished many small businesses.[14] Moreover, economic blight is often caused by government itself, which frequently deters investment and economic growth through its regulatory and tax policies. Changing those policies to give private property owners more incentive to invest is often a wiser course for fixing a blighted neighborhood. Even where the situation does call for radical alterations, they can often be pursued without forcing property owners to give up title to their land. The city of Seattle recently completed a two-year redevelopment project, which created more than a million square feet of new retail space, and did it all without resorting to eminent domain.[15]

If government does choose to use eminent domain to eliminate blight, however, it is important that legal definitions of "blight" be narrowly drawn, to prevent bureaucrats from condemning property simply because they don't like the way it's being used. Unfortunately, legal definitions of "blight" are often so broadly drawn that just about any property can qualify. The case of Lakewood, Ohio, where property was declared blighted if it lacked two-car garages or central air conditioning, is a startling example of the kinds of abuse to which blight statutes can lead. Rewording legal definitions of "blight" to allow condemnation of only truly dangerous property, or land contaminated with dangerous chemicals, would help prevent abuse.

A new law enacted in Indiana provides an excellent example of how states can protect private property rights in the wake of *Kelo*.[16] Given the fact that Indiana has seen a significant increase in eminent domain abuse in recent years, the new law signed by Gov. Mitch Daniels on March 27, 2006, is an extraordinary breakthrough. The law allows government to take property only if the property is to be possessed, occupied, and enjoyed by the general public—which allows such traditional government projects as highways or schools—or if the property is used by a public utility such as a railroad. But it prohibits the use of eminent domain for "the public benefit of economic development, including an increase in a tax base, tax revenues, employment, or general economic health." And the new law defines blight narrowly, requiring the government to show that property is a public nuisance, unfit for human habitation, dangerous to the safety of people or property, lacking in necessary utilities, undeveloped despite being in a developed area, and has become a place for the accumulation of trash, garbage, and rats. All of those factors must be present before government may seize the property, which ensures that while officials may still eliminate truly blighted property, they are not free to use the condemnation power as a tool for reshaping the local economy as they think best. Another bill, recently passed by the Pennsylvania Senate, also provides an excellent model for states to follow if they wish to prevent eminent domain abuse. S.B. 811 defines blight as abandoned or unsafe property, or property that includes abandoned wells, fire hazards, or dwellings that are "unsanitary, unsafe, vermin-infested, or . . . unfit for human habitation."[17] As with the Indiana law, the specifications in the Pennsylvania bill would bar officials from condemning property simply because they believe that it could produce more tax revenue if it were turned into a shopping center.

In addition to crafting narrow definitions of blight, it's also important to limit how government goes about declaring property blighted to begin with. One important reform for the blight statutes, for example, would be to impose a time limit on declarations of blight.

Under the laws of many states, once a property is declared blighted, that declaration never goes stale; it can remain indefinitely, allowing officials to condemn property, regardless of how the neighborhood may have improved in the interim. If the blight laws really exist to foster the improvement of dilapidated or slum areas, they should not be used to condemn property after the neighborhood has been cleaned up by other means.

Giving Property Owners Their Day in Court

State laws should allow property owners a realistic opportunity to challenge the taking of their property in court. Some states set special statutes of limitations that limit their right to appeal a blight designation to a very short amount of time and that restrict the kinds of evidence they may introduce. Although changing the rules of civil procedure may not be as dramatic as other reforms, those changes can be very important to people whose homes and businesses are taken by the state.

Another way to ensure that property owners have a realistic chance of defending their rights would be to require the government to pay attorneys' fees in condemnation cases. Under current law, the victim of a condemnation who is offered a low-ball figure as compensation must hire an attorney to challenge that figure. The property owner often must pay the lawyer a percentage of the compensation award, which means that the owner does not get the full amount of compensation for his property. Condemning agencies should be forced to pay for the citizen's attorney.

Also, in many cases, property owners are limited in the types of evidence they can present to officials deliberating over a blight designation. In one case in San Jose, California, property owner Elaine Evans lost her land even though she showed up at the city council meeting where she and more than 100 other property owners were allowed less than two minutes each to argue that their neighborhood was not blighted.[18] Worst of all, perhaps, is the tendency of courts to defer to a legislature that declares property to be blighted. Such deference is tantamount to abandoning judicial protection entirely. If property really is so blighted that it must be taken away from the owner, then legislators should have nothing to fear from an independent court evaluating the evidence. Judges should not shut their eyes to the rampant abuse of eminent domain, nor should they act as rubber stamps for city councils that declare a neighborhood blighted.

Reform is also necessary at the federal level to guarantee a realistic chance for property owners to have their cases heard in federal court. The promise of the Fourteenth Amendment was that when citizens' civil rights were violated, they could seek help from an independent federal judiciary. A series of civil rights acts sought to ensure that people who suffer from violations of their civil rights can go to federal court. But through the Court-created doctrine of the *Williamson County* case, people seeking to defend their property rights are effectively denied federal court review. To fix that problem and allow property owners their day in court requires amending federal laws, in particular the Full Faith and Credit Act. Another possibility would be to revise the Civil Rights Removal Act, a law originally intended to allow plaintiffs in civil rights suits to seek independent federal review, but which has been limited by the Supreme Court to cases involving only racial discrimination.

Also, although the Supreme Court tried to abolish the "notice rule" in the *Palazzolo* case, courts continue to rule that if a person knew (or should have known) that a land-use regulation existed before buying property, he cannot challenge its constitutionality. Judges get around the *Palazzolo* decision by employing the *Penn Central* test, declaring that a property owner's expectations of using property were "unreasonable" if the law existed at the time of purchase. To allow people to vindicate their rights in federal court, judges must be required to consider the *justice,* not the *timing,* of a challenged regulation.

Compensating People for Regulatory Takings

When government takes land outright, it usually has to pay for it. But when it regulates how a person can use—or forbids a person from using—his land, it takes away the one thing that gives the land its economic value: its *use.* While government rightly prevents people from using their land in ways that harm others, it too often exploits that power by imposing land-use restrictions that go far beyond preventing harms or nuisances and instead give the public goods at the landowner's expense. Requiring government to compensate owners for such regulatory takings would be a significant step forward in improving the protection of property rights.

Oregon's Measure 37, as discussed earlier, requires the state to compensate owners whenever the government goes beyond preventing harm and instead deprives them of the value of their property. It provides a good example of how to protect people from the excessive burdens of the regulatory state. Now that Measure 37 has been upheld by the Oregon Supreme Court, it should serve as a model for reform in other states. Even if similar laws are not passed elsewhere, the enormous popularity of Measure 37 has sent a message to government officials that they cannot expect to take things from people without just compensation, and expect the people to remain silent.

Another important legal reform would be to address what lawyers call the "relevant parcel" question. Since government is required to pay just compensation when it deprives owners of "all" of the value of their property, bureaucrats have devised clever ways of leaving landowners with a fraction of that value—allowing them to build a single home on a large parcel, for example. This loophole should be closed: government should be required to pay every time it infringes on an owner's freedom to use his land, except when it enforces traditional nuisance rules that protect neighbors' ability to use and enjoy *their* land. If a regulation deprives an owner of 10 percent of the value of his property, he should be compensated for that 10 percent loss.

You've Got to Fight for Your Right to Property

It isn't the rich who suffer most when private property rights are attacked or ignored; it's the poor and the middle class. They simply don't have the political clout to manipulate the system as do wealthy beneficiaries of eminent domain abuse like Costco. This puts homeowners and owners of small businesses at a disadvantage. Yet the groundswell against the *Kelo* decision indicates that if regular people demand change, it can happen.

Those who want to defend their right to own, use, buy, and sell private property must organize themselves. They can do so by contacting groups such as the Institute for Justice's Castle Coalition (www.castlecoalition.org), a nationwide alliance of property rights groups and regular citizens who demand protection for the things they've earned. Other organizations, including the Washington

Legal Foundation, the Mountain States Legal Foundation, the Claremont Institute, and of course the Pacific Legal Foundation, are also on the frontlines of property rights battles, and they depend on support from everyday citizens who agree with their work.

Grassroots activism is also vital. Organizing a protest march—even if it is a small one—or writing letters to the editor, or inviting speakers to address clubs or community groups can also have an important impact. Citizens should keep a close watch on their state legislatures to ensure that if an eminent domain bill is passed, it doesn't have the awful loopholes of the Texas and Alabama laws. State legislators really do listen to phone calls and letters from their constituents—if there are enough of them. And, perhaps most important, citizens must keep an eye on their city and county officials. If the city is considering condemning private property, or declaring an area "blighted," a citizen's best hope for protecting his land is to attend the city council and speak up. Often, people lose lawsuits challenging a condemnation because they fail to speak up at the right time.

If people demand reform, it can and will come. But they must not be satisfied with half-hearted measures, and they must not remain silent.

A Frequent Recurrence to Fundamental Principles

It's trite but true: the most important way to solve America's property rights crisis is through *education*. The Virginia Declaration of Rights—issued only a month before the Declaration of Independence—declared that "free government" and "the blessings of liberty" can be preserved only "by frequent recurrence to fundamental principles."[19] That is true. Only learning, understanding, and teaching others about the principles of private property and their importance in the American Constitution can solve the problems posed by eminent domain abuse, land-use regulations, and civil asset forfeiture laws. The ideas of America's Founders aren't just high-sounding rhetoric to be trotted out every Fourth of July to accompany the fireworks and apple pie; they are living, breathing principles, every bit as relevant today as they were two centuries ago. Private property is essential for happy individuals and for a prosperous, safe society. Yet today many intellectual leaders regard property rights as a superstition, or an outdated tradition, or a minor factor to be weighed

125

equally with bureaucratic notions of progress. Even the American Dream of home ownership is derided as "suburban sprawl." Without a revival of the American public's dedication to the fundamental importance of private property rights, political reforms will be fleeting.

Unfortunately, a change in the climate of ideas takes a lot longer and has effects much less immediately visible than an immediate change in the law. But ultimately, no legal reform is possible without a change in ideas. As Utah's experience with civil asset forfeiture reform demonstrates, no legal fix will be effective in the long term unless the people and, particularly, their social and political leaders believe in the change and are willing to move it forward. As Alexis de Tocqueville recognized, "[T]here is no country in which everything can be provided for by the laws, or in which political institutions can prove a substitute for common sense and public morality."[20] A nation that does not recognize—or understand—property rights is ultimately beyond redemption. Only by recognizing that there is something *necessary* about property—something innately, inextinguishably *human* and right about being able to say that something is "my own"—can we restore the American Constitution, and the American nation, to its proper order.

Notes

Chapter 1

1. Anne Rochell Konigsmark, "A Displaced Resident, Haunted by New Orleans," National Public Radio, Sept. 28, 2005. http://www.npr.org/templates/story/story.php?storyId = 4866934.

2. Homer, *The Odyssey*, trans. Robert Fagles (New York: Penguin, 1996), p. 464.

3. James Chan, *Spare Room Tycoon* (London: Nicholas Brealy, 2000), p. 5.

4. James Madison, "Property," in *James Madison: Writings*, ed. Jack Rakove (New York: Library of America, 1999), p. 515.

Chapter 2

1. Quoted in Mary Ellen Fillo, "Bugryns Take Case to Court, Fight City's Plan to Seize Property," *Hartford Courant*, Oct. 7, 1999, p. B1.

2. *Bugryn v. City of Bristol*, 2000 WL 192887, at *3 (Conn. Super. Jan. 31, 2000).

3. "It's Time Bugryns Moved Out," editorial, *Hartford Courant*, Apr. 9, 2004, p. A10.

4. Ken Byron, "Mayor's Office under Guard after Irate Telephone Call," *Hartford Courant*, Apr. 2, 2004, p. B3.

5. Quoted in Ken Byron, "Bugryn Deadline Is Tonight: City Lawyer Says Two Women in Home Have Taken No Action toward Moving," *Hartford Courant*, Apr. 1, 2004, p. B6.

6. Quoted in WFSB Bristol, "Bristol Seeks to Evict People for Industrial Park," http://www.wfsb.com/Global/story.asp?S = 954365.

7. Michael J. Dudko, e-mail to Timothy Sandefur, Nov. 20, 2004.

8. Dana Berliner, *Public Power, Private Gain: A Five-Year, State-by-State Report Examining the Abuse of Eminent Domain* (Washington: Institute for Justice, 2003).

9. Linda Cruse, "Merriam Sells Condemned Property to Baron BMW," *Kansas City Star*, Jan. 27, 1999.

10. *City of Bremerton v. Estate of Anderson*, 1999 WL 1116811 (Wash. App. Div. 2 Dec. 3, 1999), *rev. denied*, 10 P.3d 407 (Wash. 2000).

11. *Bailey v. Myers*, 206 Ariz. 224 (2003).

12. *Casino Reinvestment Development Authority v. Banin*, 320 N.J.Super. 342 (1998).

13. Jennifer J. Kruckeberg, "Can Government Buy Everything? The Takings Clause and the Erosion of the 'Public Use' Requirement," *Minnesota Law Review* 87 (2002): 543.

14. *Kelo v. City of New London*, 125 S. Ct. 2655, 2665 (2005).

15. H.R. 340 (2005).

16. *Pumpelly v. Green Bay & Mississippi Canal Co.*, 80 U.S. 166, 178 (1871) (emphasis in original).

17. J. David Breemer, "Temporary Insanity: The Long Tale of Tahoe-Sierra Preservation Council and Its Quiet Ending in the United States Supreme Court," *Fordham Law Review* 71 (2002): 1.

18. *Tahoe-Sierra Preservation Council, Inc. v. Tahoe Regional Planning Agency*, 535 U.S. 302 (2002).

19. Ibid. at 324.

20. Thomas Merrill, Testimony before the Senate Committee on the Judiciary, Sept. 20, 2005.

21. Richard Pipes, *Property and Freedom* (New York: Knopf, 2000), pp. 66–67.

22. Benjamin Spock, *Dr. Spock on Parenting: Sensible, Reassuring Advice for Today's Parent* (New York: Pocket, 1988), pp. 259–60.

23. Pipes, pp. 74–75.

24. Daniel Dennett, *Consciousness Explained* (Boston: Back Bay Books, 1992), p. 414.

25. Ibid., p. 416.

26. Daniel Dennett, *Kinds of Minds* (New York: Basic Books, 1996), pp. 138–39 (emphasis in original).

27. Virginia Postrel, *The Substance of Style* (New York: Harper Collins, 1993), p. 115.

28. "A Portrait of Jefferson Is Stolen," *Philadelphia Inquirer*, July 30, 1994, p. C12.

29. Quoted in Matt Bai, "Jefferson Portrait Recovered," *Boston Globe*, May 25, 1996, p. 13.

30. Quoted in Susan R. Stein, *The Worlds of Thomas Jefferson at Monticello* (New York: Henry N. Abrams, 1993), pp. 364–65.

31. Terry L. Anderson, "Property Rights among Native Americans," *Freeman*, Feb. 1997, http://fee.org/vnews.php?nid=3692; Terry Lee Anderson, *Not So Wild Wild West: Property Rights and Indian Economies* (Lanham, MD: Rowman & Littlefield, 1992).

32. Charles Nordoff, *Communistic Societies of the United States* (New York: Hillary House, 1875), p. 166.

33. Ibid., p. 142.

34. Dolores Hayden, *Seven American Utopias* (Cambridge, MA: MIT Press, 1976), p. 69. Among other things, Shakers were required to start with the right foot when ascending a flight of stairs and to fold their hands so that the right-hand thumb and fingers were above those on the left. A Shaker was rarely alone: two to six people shared every bedroom, and work and worship were done in groups. Members were not allowed to loiter in hallways or on doorsteps because they might find a solitary moment (p. 46). See also Nordoff, pp. 177–78.

35. Edward D. Andrews, *The People Called Shakers* (New York: Oxford University Press, 1953), pp. 178–79.

36. David R. Starbuck, "Latter-Day Shakers," *Archaeology* 52, no 1 (Jan.–Feb. 1999).

37. Stephane Courtois et al., *The Black Book of Communism* (Cambridge, MA: Harvard University Press, 1999), p. 4.

38. Pipes, p. 212.

39. Courtois et al., p. 162; Robert Conquest, *The Harvest of Sorrow: Soviet Collectivization and the Terror-Famine* (New York: Oxford University Press, 1987).

40. Juri Jelagin, *Taming of the Arts* (New York: Dutton, 1951).

41. Sheila Fitzpatrick, *Everyday Stalinism: Ordinary Life in Extraordinary Times: Soviet Russia in the 1930s* (New York: Oxford University Press, 1999), pp. 46–50.

42. Martin Malia, *The Soviet Tragedy* (New York: Free Press, 1994), p. 368.

43. Ibid., p. 225.

44. Fitzpatrick, pp. 47–48.

45. Ayn Rand, *We the Living* (New York: Signet, 1983), p. 80.

46. Philosopher Larry Arnhart concludes that "human beings generally desire the wealth necessary for a flourishing life. To satisfy this desire, every society has concepts

of property that distinguish what is owned by an individual or a group from what is owned by others. Wealth is desired to equip oneself and one's family and friends for a good life. Wealth is also desired as a display of status or prestige." Larry Arnhart, *Darwinian Natural Right* (Albany: State University of New York, 1998), p. 34.

47. Tom Bethell, *The Noblest Triumph: Property and Prosperity through the Ages* (New York: St. Martin's, 1999), p. 15.

48. Allan Bloom, "Jean-Jacques Rousseau," in *History of Political Philosophy*, ed. Leo Strauss and Joseph Cropsey, 3d ed. (Chicago: University of Chicago Press, 1987), p. 563.

49. Karl Marx, preface to *A Critique of Political Economy* (1859), in *The Marx-Engels Reader*, ed. Robert C. Tucker, 2d ed. (New York: Norton, 1978), p. 4.

50. Cass R. Sunstein, *Democracy and the Problem of Free Speech* (New York: Free Press, 1993), p. 30.

51. Frederick Douglass, *The Life and Times of Frederick Douglass*, in *Douglass: Autobiographies* (New York: Library of America, 1994), p. 634 (emphasis in original).

52. Harry V. Jaffa, *A New Birth of Freedom* (Lanham, MD: Rowman & Littlefield, 2000), pp. 112–13.

53. Thomas Jefferson, Letter to Roger Weightman, June 24, 1826, in *Jefferson: Writings*, ed. Merrill D. Peterson (New York: Library of America, 1984), p. 1517. Jefferson was paraphrasing the 17th-century writer Algernon Sidney. Jaffa, p. 111.

54. Douglass, p. 654 (emphasis in original).

55. Abraham Lincoln, Speech in Chicago, Illinois, July 10, 1858, in *Abraham Lincoln: Speeches and Writings* (New York: Library of America, 1989), p. 457.

56. John Locke, *Second Treatise of Civil Government*, ed. Peter Laslett, rev. ed. (New York: Oxford University Press, 1963), § 27 p. 329 (emphasis in original).

57. Ibid., § 135 p. 402.

58. Henry David Thoreau, *Henry David Thoreau: A Week, Walden, The Maine Woods, Cape Cod*, ed. Robert F. Sayre (New York: Library of America 1985), p. 388.

59. Nancy Friedrich, "An Old Favorite Has a New Twist," *Wireless Systems Design*, March 2005, http://www.wsdmag.com/Articles/ArticleID/9991/9991.html.

60. Norman Lebrecht, "Sony Walkman—Music to Whose Ears?" *La Scena Musicale*, July 26, 2004, http://www.scena.org/columns/lebrecht/040726-NL-walkman.html.

61. Edward Bloustein, "Group Privacy: The Right to Huddle," *Rutgers-Camden Law Journal* 8 (1977): 219.

62. Billy Graham, *Peace with God* (Garden City, NJ: Doubleday, 1953), p. 179.

63. *Cottonwood Christian Center v. Cypress Redevelopment Agency*, 218 F. Supp. 2d 1203, 1212 (C.D. Ca. 2002).

64. Ibid.

65. Ibid. at 1231.

66. Ibid.

67. Ibid. at 1232.

68. Daniel A. Farber, "Speaking in the First Person Plural: Expressive Associations and the First Amendment," *Minnesota Law Review* 85 (2001): 1483.

69. Paul Tillich, *Dynamics of Faith* (New York: Harper and Row, 1957), pp. 23–24.

70. Ibid., p. 25.

71. Ibid., p. 26.

72. *Church of Christ in Hollywood v. Superior Court*, 99 Cal. App. 4th 1244 (2002).

73. Ibid. at 1248.

74. Ibid. at 1255 (quoting *Silo v. CHW Medical Foundation*, 27 Cal. 4th 1097, 1100 (2002)).

75. *Church of Christ*, 99 Cal. App. 4th at 1257.

76. *California Democratic Party v. Jones*, 530 U.S. 567 (2000).

77. William Blackstone, *Commentaries on the Laws of England* (London: A. Strahan, 1809), vol. 1, p. 129.

78. Chan, p. 32.

79. Ibid.

80. Ibid., pp. 3–4.

81. Ibid., p. 2.

82. Answer to Petition for Writ of Mandate, *Mesdaq v. Superior Court*, Civil Case No. GIC829293-A (Cal. App. 4th Dist. Feb. 25, 2005), p. 8.

83. Quoted in Michael Gardner, "Legislators Are Rethinking Laws on Land Seizure," *Daily Breeze*, Aug. 19, 2005, p. A1.

84. Quoted in Michael Squires, "Few Gains Seen from Land Fight," *Las Vegas Review-Journal*, Aug. 15, 2004, p. 1B.

85. *City of Las Vegas Downtown Redevelopment Agency v. Carol Pappas et al.*, No. A327519 (Nev. DCA 1996) at 49a.

86. Ibid. at 51a.

87. Ibid. at 53a.

88. Ibid.

89. Ibid. at 54a.

90. Ibid. at 60a.

91. Plato, *The Republic*, in *Plato: The Collected Dialogues*, ed. Edith Hamilton and Huntington Cairns (Princeton, NJ: Princeton University Press, 1961), 5:464b–d, p. 703.

92. Plato, *Laws*, in ibid., 5:739c–e, p. 1324 (emphasis in original).

93. Aristotle, *Politics*, in *The Basic Works of Aristotle*, ed. Richard McKeon (New York: Random House, 1941), 1263b:25, p. 1152.

94. Ibid., 1263b:15, p. 1152.

95. Robert Frost, "Mending Wall" (1949), in *Robert Frost: Collected Poems, Prose, and Plays*, ed. Richard Poirier and Mark Richardson (New York: Library of America, 1995), p. 39.

96. F. A. Hayek, *Law, Legislation, and Liberty: Rules and Order* (Chicago: University of Chicago Press, 1973), vol. 1, p. 107.

97. Bethell, p. 36.

98. *The Parents' Answer Book* (New York: Roundtable, 2000), p. 237.

99. Timothy Sandefur, "A Gleeful Obituary for *Poletown Neighborhood Council v. Detroit*," *Harvard Journal of Law and Public Policy* 28 (2005): 651.

100. William A. Fischel, "The Political Economy of Public Use in *Poletown*: How Federal Grants Encourage Excessive Use of Eminent Domain," *Michigan State Law Review*, 2004, p. 929.

101. Jean Wylie, *Poletown: Community Betrayed* (Urbana: University of Illinois Press, 1990), pp. 74–75.

102. *Poletown Neighborhood Council v. Detroit*, 304 N.W.2d 455 (Mich. 1981).

103. Wylie, pp. 155–56.

104. Ibid., p. 167.

105. Ibid., pp. 219–20.

106. Robert D. Putnam, *Bowling Alone* (New York: Simon & Schuster, 2000), pp. 355–58.

107. Aristotle, 1261b:30, p. 1148.

108. Bethell, p. 10.

109. Hernando de Soto, *The Mystery of Capital* (New York: Basic Books, 2000), p. 47.

110. Ibid., p. 48.

111. Ibid., pp. 49–62.

112. Adam Smith, *An Inquiry into the Nature and Causes of the Wealth of Nations* (1776; Indianapolis: Liberty Classics, 1976), vol. 1, pp. 26–27.

113. Ludwig von Mises, *Human Action*, 3d ed. (Chicago: Regnery, 1966), pp. 327–97.

114. Ludwig von Mises, *Liberalism: The Classical Tradition* (Irvington, NY: Foundation for Economic Education, 1986), pp. 70–75.

115. Ibid., p. 72.

116. Murray N. Rothbard, "The End of Socialism and the Calculation Debate Revisited," *Journal of Austrian Economics* 5, no. 2 (1991): 74.

117. Paul Johnson, *Modern Times* (New York: Harper & Row, 1991), p. 285.

118. John Dornberg, *The Soviet Union Today* (New York: Dial, 1976), pp. 68–76.

119. Carl Brent Swisher, *Motivation and Political Technique in the California Constitutional Convention* (New York: Da Capo, 1969), p. 91.

120. Act of May 19, 1913 (California Alien Land Law) ch. 113, §§ 1–8, 1913 Cal. Stat. 206–8 (1913).

121. Keith Aoki, "No Right to Own? The Early Twentieth-Century 'Alien Land Laws' as a Prelude to Internment," *Boston College Law Review* 40 (1998): 37; Brant T. Lee, "A Racial Trust: The Japanese YWCA and the Alien Land Law," *Asian Pacific American Law Journal* 7 (2001): 12–22.

122. *Sei Fujii v. California*, 38 Cal.2d 718 (1952).

123. Iris Chang, *The Chinese in America: A Narrative History* (New York: Penguin, 2003), pp. 161–62.

124. Jeff Gillenkirk and James Motlow, *Bitter Melon* (Berkeley: Heyday Books, 1997), pp. 13–14.

125. Ibid., p. 136.

126. Ibid.

127. Quoted in Gabriel Baird, "Home at Last: Residents Finally Get to Own Land in Locke," *Sacramento Bee*, Dec. 11, 2004, p. B1.

128. Phyllis Vine, *One Man's Castle: Clarence Darrow in Defense of the American Dream* (New York: Harper Collins, 2005).

129. Ibid., p. 106.

130. Ibid., p. 107.

131. Ibid., p. 109.

132. Arthur Garfield Hays, Opening Statement of the Trial of the *People of Michigan v. Ossian Sweet et al.*, http://www.law.umkc.edu/faculty/projects/ftrials/sweet/transcriptexcerpts.HTM#Opening%20Statement.

133. Vine, pp. 190–221.

134. Charge to the Jury, *People of Michigan v. Henry Sweet*, May 13, 1926, http://www.law.umkc.edu/faculty/projects/FTrials/sweet/chargetojury.html.

135. Vine, p. 259.

136. Ibid., pp. 263–64.

137. Sunstein, p. 30.

138. Ginger Thompson, "Venezuelans Seize Warehouses," *Deseret News*, Jan. 18, 2003, p. A4.

139. Venezuelan Council for Investment Promotion, *Nuevas inversiones extranjeras por actividad económica,* http://www.conapri.org/framedetalle.asp?sec = 1102&id = 49&plantilla = 9.

140. Embassy of the United States to Kinshasa-Congo, "Investment Climate," http://kinshasa.usembassy.gov/investment_climate_.html.

141. Craig J. Richardson, "The Loss of Property Rights and the Collapse of Zimbabwe," *Cato Journal* 25, no. 3 (Fall 2005): 541, 549.

142. James Buchanan and Gordon Tullock, *The Calculus of Consent* (Ann Arbor: University of Michigan Press, 1962), p. 111.

143. Steven Greenhut, *Abuse of Power: How the Government Misuses Eminent Domain* (Santa Ana, CA: Seven Locks, 2004), pp. 198–201.

144. *99 Cents Only Stores v. Lancaster Redevelopment Agency,* 237 F. Supp. 2d 1123, 1129 (C.D.Ca. 2001).

145. Minutes of Boynton Beach City Council Meeting, April 29, 2003, pp. 1–2, http://weblink.ci.boyntonbeach.fl.us/Index.asp?DocumentID = 19751&FolderID = 14493&SearchHandle = 12868&DocViewType = ShowImage&LeftPaneType = Hidden& dbid = 0&page = 1.

146. Wendell E. Pritchett, "The 'Public Menace' of Blight: Urban Renewal and the Private Uses of Eminent Domain," *Yale Law and Policy Review* 21 (2003): 1.

147. "The Limits of Property Rights," editorial, *New York Times,* June 24, 2005, p. A22.

Chapter 3

1. Thomas Hobbes, *Leviathan,* ed. Michael Oakeshott (New York: Collier, 1962), p. 100.

2. Ibid., p. 101.

3. John Locke, *Second Treatise of Civil Government,* ed. Peter Laslett, rev. ed. (New York: Oxford University Press, 1963), § 6, p. 311.

4. Ibid., § 14, pp. 317–18.

5. Ibid., § 57, p. 348 (emphasis in original).

6. Ibid., §123, p. 395.

7. Ibid., § 135, pp. 402–3.

8. Ibid., § 138, p. 406.

9. Thomas Jefferson, Letter to Spencer Roane, Sept. 6, 1819, in *Thomas Jefferson: Writings,* ed. Merrill D. Peterson (New York: Library of America, 1984), p. 1426 (emphasis added).

10. 1 Stat. 1, 3 (1776) (emphasis added).

11. James Madison, "Sovereignty" (1835), in *Writings of James Madison,* ed. Galliard Hunt (New York: Putnam, 1910), vol. 9, pp. 570–71.

12. Locke, § 26, p. 328 (emphasis in original).

13. Thomas Jefferson, Letter to James Monroe, May 20, 1782, in *Jefferson,* p. 777.

14. Locke, § 57 pp. 347–48.

15. James Madison, "Property," in *James Madison: Writings,* ed. Jack Rakove (New York: Library of America, 1999), p. 515.

16. Thomas G. West, *Vindicating the Founders* (Lanham, MD: Rowman & Littlefield, 1997), chap. 2.

17. Tom G. Palmer, "Saving Rights Theory from Its Friends," in *Individual Rights Reconsidered,* ed. Tibor Machan (Stanford, CA: Hoover Institution Press, 2001), p. 75.

18. Quoted in Clinton Rossiter, *The Political Thought of the American Revolution* (New York: Harvest, 1963), p. 175.

19. Virginia Declaration of Rights ¶ 1 (1776).

20. John Trenchard, *Cato* no. 68, in *The Founders' Constitution,* ed. Philip Kurland and Ralph Lerner (Indianapolis: Liberty Fund, 1987), vol. 1, p. 585.

21. Thomas Jefferson, Letter to Joseph Milligan, Apr. 6, 1816, in ibid., vol. 1, p. 573.

22. James Madison, Speech in the Virginia Constitutional Convention (1830), in *James Madison,* p. 824.

23. John Adams, *Defence of the Constitution of the United States,* in *The Founders' Constitution,* vol. 1, p. 591.

24. James Wilson, "On Property," in *Works of James Wilson,* ed. Robert McCloskey (Cambridge, MA: Harvard University Press, 1967), vol. 2, p. 719.

25. Eric Claeys, "Property, Morality and Society in Founding Era Legal Treatises," Paper presented to American Political Science Association annual meeting, Aug. 30, 2002, p. 32, http://apsaproceedings.cup.org/Site/papers/068/068008ClaeysEric.pdf.

26. Magna Carta, ¶ 39 (1215).

27. James Madison, *Federalist* no. 51, in *The Federalist Papers,* ed. Clinton Rossiter (New York: New American Library, 1961), p. 322.

28. James Madison, Letter to James Monroe, Oct 5, 1786, in *The Complete Madison,* ed. Saul Padover (New York: Harper Brothers, 1953), p. 45.

29. 3 U.S. (3 Dall.) 386 (1798).

30. Ibid. at 388.

31. *VanHorne's Lessee v. Dorrance,* 28 F.Cas. 1012 (C.C.Pa. 1795) ("Every person ought to contribute his proportion for public purposes and public exigencies; but no one can be called upon to surrender or sacrifice his whole property, real and personal, for the good of the community, without receiving a recompence in value. This would be laying a burden upon an individual, which ought to be sustained by the society at large."). *Armstrong v. United States,* 364 U.S. 40, 49 (1960) ("The Fifth Amendment's guarantee that private property shall not be taken for a public use without just compensation was designed to bar Government from forcing some people alone to bear public burdens which, in all fairness and justice, should be borne by the public as a whole.").

32. Terry L. Anderson, *Sovereign Nations or Reservations? An Economic History of American Indians* (San Francisco: Pacific Research Institute, 1995); Bruce L. Benson, "Property Rights and the Buffalo Economy of the Great Plains," http://www.isnie.org/ISNIE04/Papers/Benson.pdf; Bruce L. Benson, "Enforcement of Private Property Rights in Primitive Societies: Law without Government," *Journal of Libertarian Studies* 9 (1989): 1.

33. John Ehle, *Trail of Tears* (New York: Doubleday, 1988), pp. 205–6.

34. Ibid., pp. 230–32; *Cherokee Nation v. Georgia,* 30 U.S. (5 Pet.) 1 (1831); *Worcester v. Georgia,* 31 U.S. (6 Pet.) 515 (1832).

35. *Worcester* at 559.

36. Ibid. at 561.

37. William W. Freehling, *Prelude to Civil War* (New York: Oxford University Press, 1966), p. 233; Ehle, p. 255.

38. Alf Mapp, *Thomas Jefferson: A Strange Case of Mistaken Identity* (Lanham, MD: Madison Books, 1987), pp. 406–7; Willard Sterne Randall, *Thomas Jefferson: A Life* (New York: Harper Perennial, 1994), pp. 145–48.

39. Drew McCoy, *The Last of the Fathers: James Madison and the Republican Legacy* (Cambridge: Cambridge University Press, 1991), pp. 245–47; William Lee Miller, *The Business of May Next* (Charlottesville: University Press of Virginia, 1994), pp. 171–85.

40. James Thomas Flexner, *George Washington: Anguish and Farewell 1793–1799* (Boston: Little, Brown, 1972), pp. 112–26; Joseph Ellis, *His Excellency: George Washington* (New York: Knopf, 2004), pp. 418–81.

41. Robert J. Rutland, *George Mason: Reluctant Statesman* (Baton Rouge: Louisiana State University Press, 1980), pp. 57, 86–88.

42. Thomas Jefferson, "Autobiography" (1821), in *Jefferson: Writings*, ed. Merrill D. Peterson (New York: Library of America, 1984), p. 18.

43. U.S. Const. Art V; Art I § 9 cl. 1.

44. Max Farrand, ed., *The Records of the Federal Convention of 1787* (New York: Oxford University Press, 1911), vol. 2, p. 417.

45. John P. Kaminski, ed., *A Necessary Evil? Slavery and the Debate over the Constitution* (Maple Bluff, WI: Madison House, 1995), pp. 27–71.

46. Frederick Douglass, "Bibles for Slaves," in *Frederick Douglass: Selected Speeches and Writings*, ed. Philip Foner and Yuval Taylor (Chicago: Lawrence Hill Books, 1999), p. 87 (emphasis in original).

47. Lydia Maria Child, "An Appeal in Favor of That Class of Americans Called Africans" (1833), in *Against Slavery: An Abolitionist Reader*, ed. Mason Lowrance (New York: Penguin, 2000), p. 168.

48. *Congressional Globe* 36th Cong., 1st sess., 1860, p. 2592.

49. Eric Foner, *The Story of American Freedom* (New York: Norton, 1998), p. 83.

50. http://www.etsu.edu/cas/history/docs/antislavery.htm.

51. Theodore Weld, *The Bible against Slavery* (New York: American Anti-Slavery Society, 1837), p. 20 (emphasis original).

52. *The Antelope*, 23 U.S. (10 Wheat.) 66, 120 (1825).

53. 14 Stat. 27, codified as amended at 42 U.S.C. § 1981.

54. *Barron v. Baltimore*, 32 U.S. (7 Pet.) 243 (1833).

55. Michael Kent Curtis, *No State Shall Abridge: The Fourteenth Amendment and the Bill of Rights* (Durham, NC: Duke University Press, 1986).

56. 6 F. Cas. 546, 551 (C.C.E.D. Pa. 1823).

57. Ibid. at 551.

58. Ibid. at 551–52.

59. 83 U.S. (16 Wall.) 36 (1873).

60. Timothy Sandefur, "The Right to Earn a Living," *Chapman Law Review* 6 (2003): 207.

61. *Slaughterhouse*, 83 U.S. (16 Wall.) at 96 (Field, J., dissenting).

62. See Kimberly C. Shankman and Roger Pilon, "Reviving the Privileges or Immunities Clause to Redress the Balance among States, Individuals, and the Federal Government," Cato Institute Policy Analysis no. 326, Nov. 23, 1998, p. 3, http://www.cato.org/pubs/pas/pa326.pdf.

63. *Bradwell v. Illinois*, 83 U.S. (16 Wall.) 130 (1872).

64. *United States v. Cruikshank*, 92 U.S. (2 Otto) 542 (1875).

65. *Saenz v. Roe*, 526 U.S. 489 (1999).

66. 87 U.S. (20 Wall.) 655 (1874).

67. Ibid. at 662–63. See also *Hurtado v. California*, 110 U.S. 516 535–38 (1884).

68. Ibid. at 664.

69. William Blackstone, *Commentaries on the Laws of England* (London: A. Strahan, 1809), vol. 1, p. 160.

70. Ibid., vol. 1, p. 49.

71. Ibid., vol. 1, p. 161.

72. Ibid.

73. Thomas Jefferson, Letter to James Madison, Feb. 17, 1826, in *Thomas Jefferson*, pp. 1513–14.

74. Julian S. Waterman, "Thomas Jefferson and Blackstone's Commentaries," *Illinois Law Review* 27 (1933): 650.

75. St. George Tucker, ed., *Blackstone's Commentaries* (Philadelphia: Birch and Small, 1803), vol. 1, Appendix A; vol. 2, Appendix G.

76. Ibid., vol. 1, Appendix A, p. 4.

77. Freehling, pp. 160–62, 171.

78. Randy E. Barnett, *Restoring the Lost Constitution: The Presumption of Liberty* (Princeton, NJ: Princeton University Press, 2003), pp. 253–69.

79. James Madison, "Charters," in *James Madison*, p. 502.

80. *Congressional Globe*, 30th Cong., 1st sess., 1848, pp. 872–73.

81. John C. Calhoun, *A Disquisition on Government* (1849; Indianapolis: Bobbs-Merrill, 1953), p. 6.

82. Black went on to serve as attorney general and secretary of state for President Buchanan, a position in which he served as an unembarrassed defender of slavery. Later, as a fierce opponent of Reconstruction, Black drafted President Johnson's message vetoing the Civil Rights Act of 1866.

83. *Sharpless v. Mayor of Philadelphia*, 21 Pa. 147, 160 (1853).

84. *Billings v. Hall*, 7 Cal. 1 (1857).

85. Charles Edward Merriam, *A History of American Political Theories* (New York: Macmillan, 1903), p. 310.

86. Louis Menand, *The Metaphysical Club* (New York: Farrar Straus and Giroux, 2001), p. 409.

87. *Duplex Printing Press Co. v. Deering*, 254 U.S. 443, 488 (1921) (Brandeis, J., dissenting).

88. Oliver Wendell Holmes, "Natural Law" (1918), reprinted in *The Essential Holmes*, ed. Richard Posner (Chicago: University of Chicago Press, 1992), p. 182.

89. *Truax v. Corrigan*, 257 U.S. 312, 376 (1921) (Brandeis, J., dissenting).

90. Michael McGerr, *A Fierce Discontent: The Rise and Fall of the Progressive Movement in America* (New York: Free Press, 2003), p. 286.

91. *Schenck v. United States*, 249 U.S. 47 (1919).

92. *Buck v. Bell*, 274 U.S. 200 (1927).

93. McGerr, pp. 182–218.

94. Ibid., pp. 81–89.

95. Ibid., pp. 109–11.

96. Charles Paul Freund, "Our Secret Pledge," *Reason*, June 27, 2002, http://reason.com/links/links062702.shtml; and Richard A. Epstein, *How Progressives Rewrote the Constitution* (Washington: Cato Institute, 2006), pp. 108–10.

97. *Egan v. San Francisco*, 133 P. 294, 296 (Cal. 1913).

98. McGerr, p. 166.

99. 272 U.S. 365 (1926).

100. Eric R. Claeys, "Euclid Lives? The Uneasy Legacy of Progressivism in Zoning," *Fordham Law Review* 73 (2004): 731.

101. James W. Ely Jr., "Reflections on *Buchanan v. Warley*, Property Rights, and Race," *Vanderbilt Law Review* 51 (1998): 958–59.

102. Wendell E. Pritchett, "The 'Public Menace' of Blight: Urban Renewal and the Private Uses of Eminent Domain," *Yale Law and Policy Review* 21 (2003): 47.

103. Ernest Burgess, "The Growth of the City: An Introduction to a Research Project," in *The City*, ed. Robert E. Park et al. (Chicago: University of Chicago Press, 1925), p. 54.

104. Homer Hoyt, *One Hundred Years of Land Values in Chicago* (Chicago: University of Chicago Press, 1936), p. 314.

105. Claeys, "Euclid Lives?" p. 748.

106. Arthur A. Ekirch Jr., *The Decline of American Liberalism* (New York: Athanaeum, 1976), p. 184.

107. Charles A. Beard, *An Economic Interpretation of the Constitution of the United States*, rev. ed. (New York: Free Press, 1941), pp. 324–25.

108. Howard Lee McBain, *The Living Constitution* (New York: Macmillan, 1928), p. 272.

109. Herbert Croly, *The Promise of American Life* (New Brunswick, NJ: Transaction Publishers, 1993), pp. 35–36.

110. Richard A. Epstein, *How Progressives Rewrote the Constitution* (Washington: Cato Institute, 2006).

111. Woodrow Wilson, *Constitutional Government in the United States* (New York: Columbia University Press, 1908), p. 59.

112. Dorsey Richardson, *Constitutional Doctrines of Justice Oliver Wendell Holmes* (Baltimore: Johns Hopkins University Press, 1924), p. 41.

113. Oliver Wendell Holmes, Letter to Harold Laski, Mar. 4, 1920, in *The Holmes-Laski Letters*, ed. Mark DeWolfe Howe (Cambridge: Cambridge University Press, 1953), vol. 1, p. 249.

114. Alexander Hamilton, *Federalist* no. 78, in *The Federalist Papers*, ed. Clinton Rossiter (New York: Penguin, 1968), p. 470.

115. *Lochner v. New York*, 198 U.S. 45, 76 (1905) (Holmes, J., dissenting).

116. *New State Ice Co. v. Liebmann*, 285 U.S. 262, 311 (1932) (Brandeis, J., dissenting).

117. Arthur A. Ekirch Jr., *Ideologies and Utopias: The Impact of the New Deal on American Thought* (Chicago: Quadrangle Books, 1969), p. 205.

118. Francis W. Coker, *Recent Political Thought* (New York: Appleton-Century-Crofts, 1934), p. 559.

119. Roscoe Pound, *Contemporary Legal Theory* (Claremont, CA: Claremont Colleges, 1940), p. 5.

120. Ibid., pp. 22–23.

121. Irving Brant, *Storm over the Constitution* (Indianapolis: Bobbs-Merrill, 1936), p. 242.

122. Ibid., p. 243.

123. Ibid., p. 247.

124. 291 U.S. 502 (1934).

125. *Nebbia*, 291 U.S. at 537.

126. At one time it may have been the case that laws that could not possibly accomplish their intended objectives were regulatory takings that required compensation, because they did not substantially advance a legitimate state interest. *Richardson v. Honolulu*, 124 F.3d 1150 (9th Cir. 1997). But this is no longer the case after *Lingle v. Chevron U.S.A. Inc.*, 125 S. Ct. 2074 (2005), which relegates that question to the Due Process, rather than the Takings, Clause. Under due process, such laws are subject to rational basis review where the court will employ "deference to legislative judgments about the need for, *and likely effectiveness of*, regulatory actions." *Lingle* at 2085 (emphasis added). Also, under due process it is "constitutionally irrelevant" whether "the

posited reason" for a law's function is the one Congress actually intended, *F.C.C. v. Beach Communications, Inc.,* 508 U.S. 307, 314–15, 318 (1993), or whether the legislature's choices were "unsupported by evidence or empirical data." *Beach Communications* at 315. Thus, it seems likely that a law that cannot possibly accomplish its intended objective would withstand due process scrutiny if the Court had any, even fleeting, desire to uphold it.

127. *West Coast Hotel Co. v. Parrish,* 300 U.S. 379 (1937).

128. *U.S. ex rel. Tenn. Valley Authority v. Welch,* 327 U.S. 546, 551–52 (1946).

129. *Home Building & Loan Assn. v. Blaisdell,* 290 U.S. 398 (1934).

130. Ibid. at 437.

131. 348 U.S. 26 (1954).

132. *Schneider v. District of Columbia,* 117 F. Supp. 705, 723 (D.D.C. 1953).

133. *Berman v. Parker,* 348 U.S. 26, 30 (1954).

134. Ibid. at 32–33.

135. Ibid. at 33–34.

136. "What Douglas accomplished . . . was the application of the more permissive criterion of the police power's public purpose to eminent domain." Ellen Frankel Paul, *Property Rights and Eminent Domain* (New York: Transaction Books, 1988), p. 94.

137. *Government of Guam v. Moylan,* 407 F.2d 567, 568–69 (9th Cir. 1969).

138. *Pumpelly v. Green Bay & Mississippi Canal Co.,* 80 U.S. 166, 177–78 (1871).

139. *Pennsylvania Coal Co. v. Mahon,* 260 U.S. 393, 415 (1922).

140. *Penn Central Transp. Co. v. New York City,* 438 U.S. 104 (1978).

141. Ibid. at 124.

142. Ibid.

143. *Kaiser Aetna v. United States,* 444 U.S. 164, 175 (1979).

144. Leslie Marshall Lewallen, Steven G. Geiseler, and Timothy Sandefur, "Measure 37: Paying People for What We Take," *Environmental Law* 35 (2006): 79.

145. 458 U.S. 419 (1982).

146. *Loretto,* 458 U.S. at 435–36.

147. 483 U.S. 825 (1987).

148. *Nollan,* 483 U.S. at 837.

149. Ibid. at 834 n. 3.

150. 512 U.S. 374 (1994).

151. 505 U.S. 1003 (1992).

152. Steven J. Eagle, "The Birth of the Property Rights Movement," revised, Cato Institute Policy Analysis no. 558, Dec. 15, 2005.

Chapter 4

1. Laura Oppenheimer, "Breaking Ground: Landowners Who Fought for Measure 37 Ready the First Cases," *Oregonian,* Nov. 22, 2004, p. A1.

2. Ibid.

3. *Dodd v. Hood River County,* 317 Or. 172 (1993).

4. John R. Nolon, "The National Land Use Policy Act," *Pace Environmental Law Review* 13 (1996): 519; Jerold S. Kayden, "National Land-Use Planning in America: Something Whose Time Has Never Come," *Washington University Journal of Law and Policy* 3 (2000): 448.

5. *Hawes v. State of Oregon,* No. CV-00-587-PA (U.S.D.C. Or. 2001); *Hawes v. State of Oregon,* No. 00-198 (Circuit Court for Baker County, Or., 2002).

6. James V. DeLong, *Property Matters: How Property Rights Are under Assault—And Why You Should Care* (New York: Free Press, 1997), pp. 129–30.

7. Gregory T. Broderick, "From Migratory Birds to Migratory Molecules: The Continuing Battle over the Scope of Federal Jurisdiction under the Clean Water Act," *Columbia Journal of Environmental Law* 30 (2005): 475.

8. *Quivira Min. Co. v. U.S.E.P.A.,* 765 F.2d 126, 129 (10th Cir. 1985) (emphasis added).

9. Gregory T. Broderick, "The Shifting Sands of the Clean Water Act," *Liberty,* July 2005.

10. De Long, p. 134.

11. Although the Supreme Court refused to consider Rapanos's criminal conviction, *United States v. Rapanos,* 339 F.3d 447 (6th Cir. 2003) *cert. denied,* 541 U.S. 972 (2004), it did agree to hear the appeal of his civil penalties. *United States v. Rapanos,* 376 F.3d 629 (6th Cir. 2004), *cert. granted* 126 S. Ct. 414 (2005).

12. See, e.g., *United States. v. Scott,* 424 F.3d 888, 890–91 (9th Cir. 2005), in which Judge Kozinski suggests that *Dolan* "limits the government's ability to exact waivers of rights as a condition of *benefits, even when those benefits are fully discretionary"* (emphasis added). *Dolan* involved a construction permit, which can only be described as a "fully discretionary benefit" if one has no *right* to use one's land.

13. *League of Oregon Cities v. State,* 334 Or. 645 (2002).

14. Leslie Marshall Lewallen, Steven G. Geiseler, and Timothy Sandefur, "Measure 37: Paying People for What We Take," *Environmental Law* 35 (2006): 94.

15. *MacPherson v. Department of Administrative Services,* 2006 WL 433953 (Feb 21, 2006).

16. See generally *Mugler v. Kansas,* 123 U.S. 623 (1887).

17. Richard A. Epstein, *Takings: Private Property and the Power of Eminent Domain* (Cambridge, MA: Harvard University Press, 1984) pp. 195–215.

18. *Nash v. City of Santa Monica,* 37 Cal. 3d 97, 101 n. 3 (1984).

19. Ibid. at 104.

20. George Reisman, *Capitalism: A Treatise on Economics* (Ottawa, IL: Jameson Books, 1996), pp. 253–54.

21. *Pennell v. City of San Jose,* 485 U.S. 1, 22–23 (1988) (Scalia, J., concurring and dissenting).

22. *Fred F. French Investing Co., Inc. v. City of New York,* 39 N.Y.2d 587, 596–97 (1976).

23. 445 U.S. 622 (1980).

24. *Owen,* 445 U.S. at 651–55.

25. Friedrich Hayek, *The Constitution of Liberty* (Chicago: University of Chicago Press, 1960), pp. 224–25.

26. "Median Price of a Home in California Breaks $500,000 for First Time in April, Sales Up 2.7 Percent, C.A.R. Reports," California Association of Realtors, May 24, 2005, http://www.car.org/index.php?id = MzQ5NjE = .

27. Edward L. Glaeser et al., "Why Have Housing Prices Gone Up?" *American Economic Review* (2004), available at http://post.economics.harvard.edu/faculty/glaeser/papers/Housing_Prices.pdf; "Sheltered Market," *The Economist,* Feb. 10, 2005, http://www.economist.com/finance/displayStory.cfm?story_id = 3645178.

28. John M. Quigley and Stephen Raphael, "Regulation and the High Cost of Housing in California," http://www.aeaweb.org/annual_mtg_papers/2005/0107_1430_0201.pdf.

29. James S. Burling, "Private Property Rights and the Environment after *Palazzolo*," *Boston College Environmental Affairs Law Review* 30 (2002): 1, 47, 61–62.

30. *Tahoe-Sierra Preservation Council, Inc. v. Tahoe Regional Planning Agency*, 535 U.S. 302, 335 (2002).

31. *Lingle v. Chevron U.S.A.*, 125 S. Ct. 2074 (2005).

32. *San Remo Hotel L.P. v. City and County of San Francisco*, 27 Cal. 4th 643, 695 (2002) (Brown, J., dissenting).

33. Ibid. at 695 (Brown, J., dissenting).

34. Ibid. at 651.

35. Ibid. at 677.

36. Ibid. at 671–72.

37. Ibid. at 697 (Brown, J., dissenting).

38. Ibid. at 697–98 (Brown, J., dissenting).

39. The U.S. Supreme Court later took the *San Remo* case, but only on a procedural matter, and it did not discuss the property rights issues in the case. *San Remo Hotel, L.P. v. City and County of San Francisco*, 125 S. Ct. 2491 (2005).

40. *Lake Shore & M.S.R. Co. v. Cincinnati, W. & M.R. Co.*, 19 N.E. 440, 448 (Ind. 1888).

41. Timothy Sandefur, "A Natural Rights Perspective on Eminent Domain in California: A Rationale for Meaningful Judicial Scrutiny of 'Public Use,'" *Southwestern University Law Review* 32 (2003): 659–57.

42. *State ex rel. Bruestle v. Rich*, 159 Ohio St. 13, 27 (1953).

43. Michael Malamut, "The Power to Take: The Use of Eminent Domain in Massachusetts," Pioneer Institute White Paper no. 15, Dec. 2000, pp. 7–8.

44. Bruce L. Benson, "The Mythology of Holdout as a Justification for Eminent Domain in the Public Provision of Roads," *Independent Review* 10, no. 2 (Fall 2005): 165.

45. Quoted in Steve Brown, "Dallas Man Who Refused to Sell Home to Bank Dies; House Up for Sale," *Dallas Morning News*, May 10, 2004.

46. *Poletown Neighborhood Council v. Detroit*, 410 Mich. 616 (1981).

47. Jean Wylie, *Poletown: Community Betrayed* (Urbana: University of Illinois Press, 1990), p. 230.

48. Ilya Somin, "Overcoming *Poletown: County of Wayne v. Hathcock*, Economic Development Takings, and the Future of Public Use," *Michigan State Law Review* 2004: 1107.

49. *Poletown*, 410 Mich. at 633.

50. Ibid. at 634.

51. Richard Epstein, *Takings: Private Property and the Power of Eminent Domain* (Cambridge, MA: Harvard University Press, 1985), p. 164.

52. Sandefur, "Natural Rights Perspective," pp. 600–601.

53. Thomas Cooley, *A Treatise on the Constitutional Limitations Which Rest upon the Legislative Power of the States of the America Union* (Boston: Little, Brown, 1868), p. 531.

54. 35 Mich. 333 (1877).

55. Ibid. at 339.

56. Malamut, p. 8.

57. Robert Caro, *The Power Broker* (New York: Knopf, 1974).

58. *City of Oakland v. Oakland Raiders*, 32 Cal. 3d 60 (1982).

59. 467 U.S. 986 (1984).

60. Ibid. at 1014–15.

61. 467 U.S. 229 (1984).

62. Ibid. at 240 (quoting *Berman*, 348 U.S. at 32).

63. Ibid. at 241.

64. Dana Berliner, *Public Power, Private Gain: A Five-Year, State-by-State Report Examining the Abuse of Eminent Domain* (Washington: Institute for Justice, 2003).

65. Steven Greenhut, *Abuse of Power: How the Government Misuses Eminent Domain* (Santa Ana, CA: Seven Locks, 2004), pp. 242–43.

66. Thomas Ott, "Eminent Domain Is Down but Not Dead," *Cleveland Plain Dealer*, Nov. 7, 2003, p. B3.

67. *State ex rel. Tomasic v. Unified Government of Wyandotte County/Kansas City*, 962 P.2d 543 (Kan. 1998).

68. Matt Welch, "Why the *New York Times* ♥s Eminent Domain," *Reason*, Oct. 2005, http://www.reason.com/0510/co.mw.why.shtml.

69. *West 41st Street Realty LLC v. New York State Urban Development Corp.*, 744 N.Y.S.2d 121 (N.Y.A.D. 1 Dept. 2002) *app. dismissed*, 749 N.Y.S.2d 476 (N.Y. 2002), *cert. denied*, 123 S. Ct. 1271 (2003).

70. Jim Herron Zamora, "City Forces Out 2 Downtown Businesses," *San Francisco Chronicle*, July 2, 2005, http://sfgate.com/cgi-bin/article.cgi?file/c/a/2005/07/02/BAGO4DI6GJ1.DTL.

71. Heather MacDonald, "City Playing Hardball with Businesses," *Oakland Tribune*, Nov. 18, 2004.

72. Wayne Curtis, "Brand-New Cities," *American Scholar* 75, no. 1 (Winter 2006): 113.

73. Jane Jacobs, *The Death and Life of Great American Cities* (New York: Vintage, 1992).

74. Ted Mann, "Pfizer's Fingerprints on Fort Trumbull Plan," *The Day*, Oct. 16, 2005, http://www.theday.com/eng/web/news/re.aspx?re=4f7f99ae-ffa5-4aad-88c2-65fa3c75b5e1.

75. Ibid.

76. Ibid.

77. Susette Kelo, Testimony before the Senate Committee on the Judiciary, Sept. 20, 2005.

78. Ibid.

79. *County of Wayne v. Hathcock*, 471 Mich. 445 (2004).

80. Thomas Hobbes, *Leviathan*, ed. Michael Oakeshott (New York: Collier, 1962), p. 101.

81. *Hathcock*, 471 Mich. at 482.

82. *Sharpless*, 21 Pa. at 161.

83. *Kelo*, 125 S. Ct. at 2662.

84. Ibid. at 2663.

85. *Nollan*, 483 U.S. at 834.

86. Roger Pilon, "A Court without a Compass," *New York Law School Law Review* 40 (1996): 999.

87. *Wilkinson v. Leland*, 27 U.S. (2 Pet.) 627, 658 (1829).

88. *Penn Cent. Transp. Co. v. City of New York*, 438 U.S. 104, 124 (1978).

89. *Kelo* at 2674–75 (O'Connor, J., dissenting).

90. Ibid. at 2676 (O'Connor, J., dissenting).

91. Ibid. at 2666 n. 16.

92. Ibid. at 2675 (O'Connor, J., dissenting).

93. Ibid. at 2686–87 (Thomas, J., dissenting) (quoting *United States v. Carolene Products Co.*, 304 U.S. 144, 152, n. 4 (1938)).

94. *Kelo* at 2684 (Thomas, J., dissenting).

95. Ibid. at 2684–85 (Thomas, J., dissenting).

96. Ibid. at 2681–82 (Thomas, J., dissenting).

97. Timothy Sandefur, "*Kelo*: Hope for Property Rights?" *Liberty*, Sept. 2005.

98. Cal. Health & Safety Code § 33031.

99. *Redevelopment Agency v. Rados Brothers*, 95 Cal. App. 4th 309 (2001).

100. Timothy Sandefur, "The 'Backlash' So Far: Will Citizens Get Meaningful Eminent Domain Reform?" Pacific Legal Foundation Working Paper no. 05-015, Mar. 10, 2006, available at http://papers.ssrn.com/sol3/papers.cfm?abstract_id = 868539.

101. Code of Alabama §§ 11-47-170, 11-80-1.

102. Code of Alabama § 24-2-2.

103. Mike Ward, "Eminent Domain Bill Headed to Perry," *Austin American-Statesman*, Aug. 17, 2005, http://www.statesman.com/news/content/shared/tx/legislature/stories/08/17EMINENT.html; Texas Govt. Code § 2206.001(c)(6).

104. Dan Walters, "Eminent Domain Bills Are Stalled—Except One for Casino Tribe," *Sacramento Bee*, Sept. 16, 2005, p. A3.

105. Sandefur, "Backlash," pp. 26–28.

106. Steve Kemme, "Moratorium Has Little Effect Here," *Cincinnati Enquirer*, Nov. 18, 2005, p. 2; Sandefur, "Backlash," pp. 28–31.

107. Sandefur, "Backlash," pp. 34–35.

108. 533 U.S. 606 (2001).

109. Burling, pp 1, 47, 61–62.

110. *Palazzolo v. State ex rel. Tavares*, 746 A.2d 707, 716–17 (R.I. 2000).

111. *Palazzolo*, 533 U.S. at 627.

112. See, e.g., *George Washington University v. District of Columbia*, 391 F. Supp. 2d 104, 113 4 (D.D.C., 2005).

113. *Williamson County Regional Planning Comm'n v. Hamilton Bank of Johnson City*, 473 U.S. 172 (1985).

114. *San Remo Hotel, L.P. v. City and County of San Francisco*, 125 S. Ct. 2491 (2005).

115. Ibid. at 2509 (Rehnquist, J., concurring).

116. Michael M. Berger, "Supreme Bait & Switch: The Ripeness Ruse in Regulatory Takings," *Washington University Journal of Law and Policy* 3 (2000): 99.

117. Eric Blumenson and Eva Nilsen, "Policing for Profit: The Drug War's Hidden Economic Agenda," *University of Chicago Law Review* 65 (1998): 35.

118. Roger Pilon, "Forfeiting Reason," *Regulation* 19, no. 3 (Fall, 1996).

119. Henry Hyde, *Forfeiting Our Property Rights* (Washington: Cato Institute, 1995), pp. 6–7.

120. Blumenson and Nilsen, p. 40.

121. Scott Ehlers, *Policy Briefing: Asset Forfeiture* (Washington: Drug Policy Foundation, 1999), p. 6.

122. *United States v. $506,231 in U.S. Currency*, 125 F.3d 442 (7th Cir. 1997).

123. Ibid. at 454 (quoting *United States v. All Assets of Statewide Auto Parts, Inc.*, 971 F.2d 896, 905 (2d Cir. 1992)).

124. *State ex rel. Wayne County Prosecuting Attorney v. Bennis*, 200 Mich.App. 670, 674 (Mich.App. 1993).

125. *Michigan ex rel. Wayne County Prosecutor v. Bennis*, 447 Mich. 719, 740 (1994).

126. *Bennis v. Michigan*, 516 U.S. 442, 449 (1996).

127. Ibid. at 446–47 (quoting *The Palmyra*, 25 U.S. (12 Wheat.) 1, 14 (1827)).

128. Evan Williford, "The Basics of Forfeiture: Testing the Limits of Constitutionality," *Criminal Justice*, Winter 2000, p. 26.

129. *Jones v. U.S. Drug Enforcement Admin.*, 819 F. Supp. 698, 724 (M.D. Tenn. 1993).

130. Leonard W. Levy, *A License to Steal: The Forfeiture of Property* (Chapel Hill: University of North Carolina Press, 1996), pp. 4–5; "Victims of Raids Have No Recourse," *Washington Times*, June 16, 1993, p. A5.

131. Office of District Attorney, Ventura County, California, "Report on the Death of Donald Scott," Mar. 30, 1993, http:// www.fear.org/chron/scott.txt.

132. 18 U.S.C. § 981.

133. Brant C. Hadaway, "Executive Privateers: A Discussion on Why the Civil Asset Forfeiture Reform Act Will Not Significantly Reform the Practice of Forfeiture," *University of Miami Law Review* 55 (2000): 87.

134. Institute for Justice, "Ending Prosecution for Profit in Utah: Citizens Demand Prosecutors Follow State's Civil Forfeiture Law," http://www.ij.org/private_property/ utah/backgrounder.html.

135. *Kennard v. Leavitt*, 246 F. Supp. 2d 1177 (D. Utah 2002).

136. Kirsten Stewart, "Seized Assets Are Pocketed," *Salt Lake Tribune*, Jan. 25, 2003, p. 1; Kirsten Stewart, "Seized Money Stuck in Counties," *Salt Lake Tribune*, Apr. 29, 2004.

137. Scott Bullock, "IJ Helps End Utah's Prosecution for Profit" *Liberty & Law*, Oct. 2003, http://www.ij.org/publications/liberty/2003/12_5_03_c.html.

138. Jennifer Dobner, "Lawmakers Overturn 2000 Forfeiture Law," *Deseret Morning News*, Mar. 3, 2004, p. B6; "Contempt for the Voters," *Salt Lake Tribune*, Mar. 6, 2004.

139. *Dolan v. City of Tigard*, 512 U.S. 374, 392 (1994).

140. Greenhut, *Abuse of Power*, p. 196.

141. This famous line is not recorded in the official court reports; it was recorded by a member of the courtroom audience. Dean L. Kinvin Wroth, "The Law as a Public Profession," *Vermont Law Review* 21 (1996): 376 n. 3.

142. J. David Breemer, "What Property Rights? The California Coastal Commission's History of Abusing Land Rights and Some Thought on the Underlying Causes," *UCLA Journal of Environmental Law and Policy* 22 (2004): 289–92.

143. Peter Douglas, "Shades of Green: Buying and Selling Environmental Protection," speech delivered at Environmental Law Conference, Yosemite, CA, Oct. 26, 2002, p. 2 (on file with author).

143. Ibid.

145. Steven Greenhut, "Going Coastal," *Orange County Register*, Feb. 2, 2003; Terry Rodgers, "Bucking the Tide: Coastal Commission's Executive Director Not Afraid to Take on Friend or Foe to Realize His Vision for Protecting California's 1,100 Miles of Precious Seashore," *San Diego Union-Tribune*, June 5, 2005, p. A1.

146. Douglas, "Shades of Green," p. 6.

147. Ibid., p. 7.

148. Ibid., p. 11.

149. Ibid., p. 15.

150. Ibid., p. 2.

151. Peter Douglas, "Environmental Politics on Uncommon Ground," speech delivered at Planning and Conservation League Conference, Sacramento, Feb. 2, 2002, p. 5 (on file with author).

152. Ibid., p. 3.

153. Douglas, "Shades of Green," pp. 8–9.

154. *Schneider v. California Coastal Commission*, No. CV-040488 (San Louis Obispo County, June 30, 2005).

155. Quoted in David Sneed, "County Leads in View Protection Trend," *San Luis Obispo Tribune,* Aug. 8, 2005.

156. *Semayne's Case,* 77 Eng. Rep. 194 (K.B. 1604).

157. Brian Martinez, "Not in Their Back Yard?" *Orange County Register,* May 10, 2004, http://www2.ocregister.com/ocrweb/ocr/article.do?id=94312&section= LOCAL&subsection=LOCAL&year=2004&month=5&day=10.

158. *Healing v. California Coastal Com.,* 22 Cal. App. 4th 1158, 1168 (1994).

159. Ibid. at 1168.

160. Breemer, "What Property Rights?" pp. 271–72.

Chapter 5

1. H.R. 4128 (2005).

2. William Fischel, "The Political Economy of Public Use in *Poletown:* How Federal Grants Encourage Excessive Use of Eminent Domain," *Michigan State Law Review* 2005: 955.

3. *County of Wayne v. Hathcock,* 471 Mich. 445 (2004).

4. *Southwestern Illinois Development Authority v. National City Environmental, L.L.C.,* 199 Ill.2d 225 (2002).

5. Wash. Const. Art I § 16; Ariz. Const. Art II § 17.

6. *Manufactured Housing Communities of Washington v. State,* 142 Wash.2d 347, 370–74 (2000); *Bailey v. Myers,* 206 Ariz. 224 (2003).

7. *HTK Management v. Seattle Popular Monorail Authority,* 2005 WL 2709354 (Oct. 20, 2005). Arizona courts, too, have carved out an exception allowing condemnation for certain redevelopment projects. See Benjamin Barr et al., "This Land Is My Land: Reforming Eminent Domain after *Kelo v. City of New London,*" Goldwater Institure Policy Brief 06–01, Jan. 17, 2006.

8. SCA 15 (2005).

9. Dan Walters, "Eminent Domain Bills Are Stalled—Except One for Casino Tribe," *Sacramento Bee,* Sept. 16, 2005, http://www.sacbee.com/content/politics/story/ 13572792p-14413211c.html.

10. *Hathcock,* 471 Mich. at 473–75.

11. Timothy Sandefur, "The 'Backlash' So Far: Will Citizens Get Meaningful Eminent Domain Reform?" Pacific Legal Foundation Working Paper no. 05-015, Jan. 25, 2006, pp. 140–41, available at http://papers.ssrn.com/sol3/papers.cfm?abstract_ id=868539.

12. http://www.castlecoalition.org/legislation/model/state_constitution.asp.

13. http://www.reason.org/eminentdomain/EminentDomain_StateStatutoryLanguage. pdf.

14. Ilya Somin, "Overcoming *Poletown: County of Wayne v. Hathcock,* Economic Development Takings, and the Future of Public Use," *Michigan State Law Review* 2004: 1016–18.

15. Mark Brnovich, "Condemning Condemnation: Alternatives to Eminent Domain," Goldwater Institute Policy Report no. 195, June 14, 2004, http://www. goldwaterinstitute.org/pdf/materials/454.pdf.

16. House Enrolled Act 811, available at http://www.in.gov/legislative/bills/ 2006/HE/HE1010.1.html.

17. S.B. 811 § 205(b).

18. *Evans v. City of San Jose,* 128 Cal. App. 4th 1123 (2005).

19. Virginia Declaration of Rights, ¶ XV (1776).

20. Alexis de Tocqueville, *Democracy in America*, trans. George Lawrence (1848; New York: Harper Perennial, 1969), p. 122.

Bibliography on Property Rights

The literature on property rights and the many issues surrounding them is vast. This list includes only a few of the works best suited for the average reader. Left out are many of the better-known classics, such as John Locke's *Second Treatise of Civil Government*, because readers who want to explore the issues of property rights more can learn about such important classics by following the leads they find in the following books. I have marked with an asterisk those books I consider particularly useful for laymen or those new to the subject.

Barnett, Randy. *The Structure of Liberty: Justice and the Rule of Law*. Oxford: Oxford University Press, 1998. Barnett provides a sophisticated philosophical defense of the necessity of individual liberty (including the liberty to own and use property) for human success and flourishing.

Barzel, Yoram. *Economic Analysis of Property Rights*. Cambridge: Cambridge University Press, 1997.

*Berliner, Dana. *Public Power, Private Gain: A Five-Year, State-by-State Report Examining the Abuse of Eminent Domain*. Washington: Institute for Justice, 2003. The most comprehensive report available on the abuse of eminent domain by government to benefit private interest groups.

*Bethell, Tom. *The Noblest Triumph: Property and Prosperity through the Ages*. New York: St. Martin's, 1999. An elegantly written and entertaining look at private property from a historical and economic perspective.

Block, Walter, and Edgar Olsen. *Rent Control: Myths and Realities*. Vancouver: Fraser Institute, 1981.

Bolick, Clint. *Leviathan*. Stanford, CA: Hoover Institution, 2004. In chapter 5, Bolick, cofounder of the Institute for Justice, describes some of the institute's victories against eminent domain abuse.

Coase, Ronald H. *The Firm, the Market, and the Law*. Chicago: University of Chicago Press, 1988. A classic examination of the economic effects of private property rights, including works that won Coase the Nobel Prize in economics.

*DeLong, James V. *Property Matters: How Property Rights Are under Assault—And Why You Should Care*. New York: Free Press, 1997. De Long's book covers every aspect of the present-day crackdown on private property rights, from regulatory takings to eminent domain. An excellent introduction for the layman, this book is full of shocking stories of government overreaching.

Eagle, Steven J. "The Birth of the Property Rights Movement." Cato Institute Policy Analysis no. 558, revised Dec. 15, 2005. Eagle explains why recent decades have seen a backlash against government's exploitation of private property owners.

Eggertsson, Thrain. *Economic Behavior and Institutions*. Cambridge: Cambridge University Press, 1991.

Ely, James W. Jr. *The Guardian of Every Other Right: A Constitutional History of Property Rights*. Oxford: Oxford University Press, 1998.

Epstein, Richard A. *How Progressives Rewrote the Constitution*. Washington: Cato Institute, 2006. An excellent brief introduction to the intellectual revolution that laid the groundwork for many of today's abuses of private property rights.

———. *Simple Rules for a Complex World*. Cambridge, MA.: Harvard University Press, 1995.

———. *Takings: Private Property and the Power of Eminent Domain*. Cambridge, MA: Harvard University Press, 1985. A classic examination of the economic and constitutional issues surrounding eminent domain. One of the most important books ever written in constitutional law, *Takings* can be a difficult book for the layman.

Friedman, David D. *Law's Order: What Economics Has to Do with Law and Why It Matters*. Princeton, NJ: Princeton University Press, 2000.

*Greenhut, Steven. *Abuse of Power: How the Government Misuses Eminent Domain*. Santa Ana, CA: Seven Locks, 2004. Greenhut, a reporter for the *Orange County Register*, documents many recent cases of government using eminent domain to benefit private lobbyists, such as Costco, at the expense of property owners.

Machan, Tibor R., ed. *Individual Rights Reconsidered*. Stanford, CA: Hoover Institution, 2001. Four brief essays on the history and philosophy of individual rights. Particularly important is Douglas Den Uyl and Douglas Rasmussen's explanation of why a libertarian society is not an immoral one.

*von Mises, Ludwig. *Liberalism: The Classical Tradition*. Irvington, NY: Foundation for Economic Education, 1996. An excellent brief introduction to the work of this extremely important economist, *Liberalism* has a particularly good introduction to the important role that prices play in an economy.

O'Driscoll, Gerald P. Jr., and W. Lee Hoskins. "Property Rights: The Key to Economic Development," Cato Institute Policy Analysis no. 482, Aug. 7, 2003.

Paul, Ellen, Fred Miller Jr., and Jeffrey Paul, eds., *Property Rights*. Cambridge: Cambridge University Press, 1994.

*Pipes, Richard. *Property and Freedom*. New York: Knopf, 2000. The best recent book on private property, despite some digressions. Pipes, who specializes in the history of the Soviet Union, is particularly good at describing how the lack of a theory of property rights explains the historical crises faced by Russia.

*Rand, Ayn. *Capitalism: The Unknown Ideal*. New York: Signet, 1968. A thorough account of the moral justification of private property rights and economic liberty.

Rosenberg, Nathan, and L. E. Birdzell Jr. *How the West Grew Rich: The Economic Transformation of the Industrial World*. New York: Basic Books, 1986.

Siegan, Bernard H. *Property and Freedom*. New Brunswick, NJ: Transaction, 1997. Siegan carefully documents the reasons for constitutional protection of private property and the ways in which the Supreme Court has abandoned those protections.

———. *Property Rights: From Magna Carta to the Fourteenth Amendment*. New Brunswick, NJ: Transaction, 2001.

*De Soto, Hernando. *The Mystery of Capital: Why Capitalism Triumphs in the West and Fails Everywhere Else*. New York: Basic Books, 2000. A brilliant, readable explanation of the importance of property law structures in advancing economic development.

Vine, Phyllis. *One Man's Castle: Clarence Darrow in Defense of the American Dream*. New York: Harper Collins, 2004. Vine's book is a dramatic account of one of the lesser-known struggles of this civil rights pioneer.

Index

public benefit synonymous with
public use, 94, 100, 103
public use, implication, 94
reforms, 123–24
Williamson County trap, 108, 123
Public Use Clause, 93, 95, 99, 103–4

Quigley, John M., 87

racial discrimination, 39–43, 47–48,
68–69, 123
Rados Brothers, "future blight"
condemnation, 105
railroad construction, 92–94, 104, 119
decisionmaking example, 38, 45
Rand, Ayn, 17
Rapanos, John, 81
Raphael, Steven, 87
rational basis test/rational relationship
standard, 73, 88, 89
Reason Foundation, model
constitutional amendments, 119–20
redevelopment/revitalization. *See*
urban planning/renewal
reforms
blighted areas, 120–22
change in ideas and, 126
Civil Asset Forfeiture Reform Act,
111–12
civil procedure, 122–23
demanding, 124–25
eminent domain, 117–20
just compensation, 123–24
post-*Kelo* legislative reforms, 105–6
regulatory takings, 8, 75–76, 79–90
reforms, 123–24
Rehnquist, William, 108, 110, 117
Reisman, George, 84
relationships
group identification and, 24–27, 48
individual sphere of privacy and,
22–24
law of trespass and, 19–20, 43
relevant parcel/denominator problem,
88, 124
religious groups, 24–27
rent control, 83–85
rent seeking, 45–48, 112
Rhode Island, 88
Palazzolo v. Rhode Island, 107–8, 123
Richardson, Bill, 106
Richardson, Craig J., 44
"the right to huddle," 24–27
Roberts, Owen, 73

Rodriguez, Ramon, 91
Roosevelt, Theodore, 68
Rousseau, Jean-Jacques, 17–19
Rowland, John, 99
Ruckelshaus v. Monsanto, 95, 102
Ryan, James, 94
Ryerson v. Brown, 94

Sacramento Housing and Development
Authority, 40
San Remo Hotel, 88–89, 108
savings and investment, 2, 29–31, 48,
49
Scalia, Antonin, 77, 85
Scott, Donald, 111
Second Treatise on Civil Government, 22
security, financial, 2, 4, 29–31, 48
security of property rights, 38
lack of, 44–48
self-defense, 51–52
self-expression. *See* individuality, self-
sufficiency, and independence
self-interest, 36–37
self-ownership, 21–22, 53–55, 61–62,
65–66
Senate testimony, 8–9
"sentimental value," 1, 12–14, 48
Shakers, abolition of private property,
14–15
sic utere tuo ut alienum non laedas, 81
60 Minutes, Lakewood, Ohio, story, 96
Slaughterhouse Cases, 63
slavery, 21–22, 59, 60–62, 65–66
small business
economic independence, 27–29
fighting for rights, 124–25
Smith, Adam, 36–37
Smith, Roger, 33
social responsibility, 35
society/societies
"as a whole," 18
benefits of property to, 31–38, 49, 56
civil tension and violence, 39–44, 48,
51–52
civility and respect, 32–34, 48
"good fences" principle, 32, 39, 48,
49
life without private property, 39–49
"live and let live" principle, 32
ownership and, 18, 32
prices and "economic calculation"
and, 37–38
primitive communism, 18–19
property rights among, 14–20

153

About the Author

Timothy Sandefur is a staff attorney at the Pacific Legal Foundation, a nonprofit organization dedicated to defending property rights and economic liberty. The foundation has defended property owners in many of the cases described in this book, including *Nollan v. California Coastal Commission, Healing v. California Coastal Commission, Palazzolo v. Rhode Island, Rapanos v. United States, Mesdaq v. San Diego, Tahoe-Sierra v. Tahoe Regional Planning Agency, Dolan v. City of Tigard, MacPherson v. Department of Administrative Services, Wayne County v. Hathcock, San Remo Hotel v. San Francisco, Hawaii Housing v. Midkiff,* and *Kelo v. New London,* in which Sandefur represented the Bugryn and Pappas families. Sandefur has written extensively on eminent domain, including articles for the *Washington Times, National Review Online,* and the *Harvard Journal of Law and Public Policy.* A graduate of Hillsdale College and Chapman University School of Law, Sandefur was recently awarded a Ronald Reagan Medal by the Claremont Institute for his work in public interest law. He lives in Rescue, California.

Cato Institute

Founded in 1977, the Cato Institute is a public policy research foundation dedicated to broadening the parameters of policy debate to allow consideration of more options that are consistent with the traditional American principles of limited government, individual liberty, and peace. To that end, the Institute strives to achieve greater involvement of the intelligent, concerned lay public in questions of policy and the proper role of government.

The Institute is named for *Cato's Letters*, libertarian pamphlets that were widely read in the American Colonies in the early 18th century and played a major role in laying the philosophical foundation for the American Revolution.

Despite the achievement of the nation's Founders, today virtually no aspect of life is free from government encroachment. A pervasive intolerance for individual rights is shown by government's arbitrary intrusions into private economic transactions and its disregard for civil liberties.

To counter that trend, the Cato Institute undertakes an extensive publications program that addresses the complete spectrum of policy issues. Books, monographs, and shorter studies are commissioned to examine the federal budget, Social Security, regulation, military spending, international trade, and myriad other issues. Major policy conferences are held throughout the year, from which papers are published thrice yearly in the *Cato Journal*. The Institute also publishes the quarterly magazine *Regulation*.

In order to maintain its independence, the Cato Institute accepts no government funding. Contributions are received from foundations, corporations, and individuals, and other revenue is generated from the sale of publications. The Institute is a nonprofit, tax-exempt, educational foundation under Section 501(c)3 of the Internal Revenue Code.

CATO INSTITUTE
1000 Massachusetts Ave., N.W.
Washington, D.C. 20001
www.cato.org